A
CARTOON HISTORY
OF ARCHITECTURE

Here is architecture not only without tears but with wit and immediacy. Osbert Lancaster takes us on a tour of the exteriors and interiors (furnishings, fashions and all) of buildings from the stone age to skyscrapers and high-risers. He enables us to catch glimpses of life as it was lived in the different periods and changing surroundings. *A Cartoon History of Architecture* is a duet between text and illustration each as witty and inform-ative as the other.

This book is a new edition, with additions, of Osbert Lancaster's classic *Here, of All Places*, which combined his original *Pillar to Post* and *Homes Sweet Homes* together with the American scene.

'Around none of the arts with the possible exceptions of dry-fly fishing and twelve-tone music has so formid-able a mystique been woven as that which befogs architecture.' (Osbert Lancaster)

'Superb; so full of such lively wit. Deep learning is combined with gay epigrams.' (*The Observer*)

OTHER WORKS BY OSBERT LANCASTER

A CARTOON
HISTORY OF
ARCHITECTURE

OSBERT LANCASTER

Illustrated by the Author

ENLARGED EDITION

JOHN MURRAY

First edition
(combining *Pillar to Post* and *Homes Sweet Homes*
with additional American subjects and published
under the title *Here, of All Places)* 1959
Second edition
(with additions and new title) 1975
Reprinted 1983
©Osbert Lancaster 1959 and 1975

Printed in Hong Kong by Kings Time Printing Press Ltd.
and published by
John Murray, Albemarle Street, London
Paperback 0 7195 3244 2

To
KAREN

AUTHOR'S NOTE

All the architecture in this book is completely imaginary, and no reference is intended to any actual building living or dead.

CONTENTS

" The art of architecture studies not structure in itself, but the effect of structure on the human spirit."

GEOFFREY SCOTT.

ORDER TO VIEW

AROUND none of the arts, with the possible exceptions of dry-fly fishing and twelve-tone music, has so formidable a mystique been woven as that which befogs architecture. From Ruskin onwards architectural writers have not hesitated either to expand their subject to cover a variety of moral and sociological themes for which the pretext was not immediately, or indeed subsequently, obvious ; or else so to isolate it from the rest of human experience as to render it for the ordinary reader as remote and incomprehensible as the quantum theory. Both these attitudes are the result of an inferiority complex induced by the very nature of architecture, half art, half science. A century ago architects were hagridden by the fear lest they be thought less " creative," artistically speaking, and therefore less socially acceptable, than painters or musicians : today they are scared stiff lest they be considered less realist than engineers.

The confusion thus induced in the mind of the public seemed to me twenty years ago, when the slim volumes of which the present work is an expansion first appeared, and still seems, wholly deplorable ; for with none of the arts is the layman so inescapably involved as with architecture. He is not compelled, provided he is a bachelor and can still turn a knob, to listen to Hindemith or Count Basie ; it is still, just, possible to go through life without ever consciously seeing a Picasso ; no compulsion as yet exists, anyhow this side of the curtain, to read Auden or buy a ticket for Sartre. But architecture is always with us ; we sit in it, work in it, and pass by whole chunks of it every day. Only Red Indians and troglodytes can completely escape its unvarying pressure. My object, therefore, was twofold. First, to do for buildings what so many popular writers have done for birds, to render them a source of informed interest and lively excitement for the passer-by so that his quiet satisfaction at having identified a nice bit of Bankers' Georgian might equal that of the keen bird-watcher on having spotted a red-breasted fly-catcher ; second, and with no very sanguine hopes of achievement, that such an interest, once stimulated, might become so widespread as to cause inconvenience to speculative builders, borough surveyors, government departments and other notorious predators.

During the last two decades much has happened, at least in England, to further my purpose. The war and its aftermath enforced the realization that while architecture might well be, as Goethe so succinctly put it, frozen music it has, nevertheless, an unfortunate tendency to melt. As the number of masterpieces, and agreeable run-of-the-mill examples, of the architecture of the past was steadily reduced by the activities first of the Luftwaffe and then of the Church Commissioners, the Ministry of Transport and other bureaucratic juggernauts, so did their value in the eyes of the public increase. At the same time a worthy eagerness, not perhaps in every case entirely unconnected with economic developments, inspired an ever-increasing number of stately-homeowners to share, on certain days, their treasures with the public at large. Furthermore the eloquence and enthusiasm of such speakers as Mr. Betjeman and Sir John Summerson brought architecture increasingly to the notice of the listening millions, and have done much to extirpate some once popular errors of taste. Thus the antiquarian heresy, first denounced by Mr. Betjeman, has lost much of its power to harm. Merit is no longer determined solely by age, and Gothic is not now invariably exalted at the expense of Georgian. And the resultant urge to put every building, no matter how contemporary its purpose, into period fancy dress is likewise on the wane.

New myths, however, have not been lacking to replace the old and to colour sound judgement. It has come to be widely believed, for instance, that some peculiar redeeming merit lies in extreme simplicity, and whereas in earlier times it was piously hoped that a bad design could be redeemed by an abundance of ill-conceived ornament it is now held for gospel that a total absence of trimmings will automatically insure a good one. The Keatsian confusion of truth and beauty is more widespread than ever, so that while the architectural merits (such as they are) of Michael Angelo's dome are briskly discounted on the grounds that the whole thing is held together by a concealed chain, unstinted praise is accorded some dreary office block solely on the grounds that its supremely uninteresting method of construction is clearly apparent to every casual passer-by. Functionalism, that arose as an understandable and, in the main, praiseworthy reaction against nineteenth-century architectural fancy dress, has been exalted into a dogma so that now nothing is ever left to our imagination and we are all forced, whether we want to or not, to watch the dullest conceivable wheels go round. Enlightened public opinion, it is clear, is not yet so powerful that either architects or their patrons can with any safety be left unwatched for more than a few seconds.

Nevertheless my primary purpose is neither didactic nor propagandist. The present expanded volume remains like its predecessors " primarily a picture-book and the letterpress is intended to do no more than provide a small mass of information leavened by a large dose of personal prejudice." In the twenty years that have elapsed since these words were written I am all too conscious of having grown much older but have no confidence at all that I am become any the wiser, so that youthful prejudices have been left unaltered even though they have in some cases been modified or flatly contradicted by those acquired in middle age. Thus I no longer find nineteenth-century Gothic so invariably funny as once I did and knowledge has only served to increase my admiration for such men as Butterfield, Pearson and H. H. Richardson. Ruskin I hold to be a far finer (although still infinitely dangerous) writer than the casual references to him in the present work might lead the reader to suspect. And age has brought increased appreciation of many works both in the Perpendicular and the Elizabethan styles. On the other hand closer acquaintance has reinforced the opinion that it is very lucky for the Romans that the majority of their buildings are only known to us in an advanced state of ruin.

In one respect, however, the years have undeniably brought increase of knowledge. When *Pillar to Post* first appeared American architecture, even that of the Eastern seaboard, was for me, as it has remained for the majority of my fellow-countrymen, *terra incognita*. The nodding acquaint-ance subsequently acquired, brief and inadequate as it has been, is still sufficient to encourage me to some small attempt to fill the gap, and most of the fresh material in the present volume was conceived with this purpose.

To the English reader two things about American architecture may well come as a surprise, as indeed they did to the author : first, that there is so much of it, particularly of the eighteenth and early nineteenth centuries, and in most cases so well preserved ; and, second, that it is, even of the earliest period, so subtly but yet so unequivocally different. This realization, although chastening, is long overdue.

To the American the treatment by a foreigner of a subject with which he may be pardoned for considering himself already sufficiently familiar may perhaps be justified on the grounds that the national attitude, in this respect, or so it seems to me, occasionally errs on the side of insufficient appreciation. Overawed by the lofty pretensions of the innumerable *kunstforcher* who have come to roost on his shores his response to architecture is too often coloured by a high seriousness that excludes from his considera-tion, as in some way unworthy, some of the less pretentious of his country's buildings.

For architecture, it cannot be said too often, is not confined to temples, palaces, state capitols, churches and public libraries ; the term extends, and with equal force, to drugstores, tram-depots, comfort stations and saloons. (The fact that so many of the latter do not, in fact, qualify as architecture results not from their function but their design.) And as it is in architecture that the surest, if still uncertain, guide to the character and achievements of extinct civilizations is to be found, so the testimony of these despised and unconsidered structures is likely to carry as much weight with future generations as that of more pompous and generally acclaimed undertakings. " Time which antiquates Antiquities, and hath an art to make dust of all things, hath yet spared these minor monuments." Scholars two millennia hence are as likely to base their speculations on the remains of Jo's Diner as on the ruins of Grant's Tomb.

Equally, architecture is not to be confined solely to exteriors, for the distinction drawn between it and interior decoration is arbitrary and inexact. The living-room, whether cathedral-ceilinged, open-planned or just plain cosy is as much architecture as the façade and for this reason I have not hesitated to include comparative studies of interiors. Apart from what one hopes is their intrinsic interest their inclusion seemed to me to be justified on the grounds that they might perhaps serve to humanize the whole subject and to reinforce the lesson that architecture does not exist, and is not to be studied, in a vacuum ; that its full significance is only to be appreciated in relation to the daily life, the aspirations and the ideals of those it was created to shelter or amuse. For it is not, like orchids or skiing, of its very nature exotic in all but a few climatically favoured localities, and while it is true that many of its greatest achievements adorn such well-publicized sites as the Acropolis or the Bosphorus or the Ile de France, it is subject to no geographical limitations and flourishes, or could flourish, equally well right here.

O. L.

xvi

A
CARTOON HISTORY
OF ARCHITECTURE

WHEN the rude forefathers of Western Civilization, towards the end of the second millennium B.C., first came sweeping down into the Mediterranean world they were still, to all intents and purposes, in the wigwam stage. The average family occupied, admittedly for short periods, a circular hole in the ground surrounded by a low dry-stone wall on top of which was erected a tent-type roof of pine branches. (Similar shelters are to-day inhabited during the summer by Vlach nomads in many parts of Greece.) But the Minoan householders whom they displaced were living in highly developed, split-level residences complete with the best plumbing which Europe was to know for more than three thousand years, of which the plans can be reconstructed with a certain degree of accuracy but of which the elevations remain a matter for speculation. (This has not, of course, deterred numerous archaeologists from producing any number of the most detailed restorations.)

From the residents the newcomers borrowed little save the flat lintel supported by wooden pillars. The art of thatching having developed fairly naturally from the old pine-branch roof they were able before long to evolve a simple formula for larger buildings by combining an open porch, supported on pillars over the entrance, with the semi-circular end derived from the original pit-dwellings. This was known as the *megaron* and is the direct ancestor of all subsequent places of assembly from the Parthenon to Coventry Cathedral.

In the course of time the original dry-stone walls were replaced by walls of brick or dressed stone, still unmortared until very late in classical times, and the roof was covered in tiles which involved an abandonment of the apsidal end as the technical difficulties of covering a semi-circular roof with tiles remained insurmountable for several centuries to come. Gradually timber, always at a premium in the Hellenic world, was abandoned in favour of stone, but various traces of the technique involved in wooden construction, such as the projecting beam-ends with their securing pegs, were retained as decorative adjuncts carried out in stone for as long as the Doric style continued to flourish. Thus early, heedless of what Messrs. Corbusier and Gropius were going to say, did the first, though not perhaps the least accomplished, of European architects light-heartedly compromise with the strict principles of structural truth.

2

"THERE was no passion in this architecture," remarks a modern traveller, recording his impressions of the Parthenon, "it was like a complicated and varying formula in three dimensions that is so very easy when you know how." Which sums up very neatly the three great characteristics of the first of the world's great architectural styles ; its apparent simplicity, its actual complexity and the rigidly intellectual basis on which it rests. It was a method of building in wood that had been adapted, and successfully adapted, to construction in stone. The basis of the style was the lintel, that is to say, the horizontal wooden beam resting on two or more uprights, but on this simple foundation has been raised the subtlest, the most complete and the most purely logical style of architecture that the world has ever known.

It is customary to speak of the three Orders of Greek architecture —the Doric, the Ionic and the Corinthian—each of which while differing in such details as the moulding of the cornice, the decoration of the entablature and the form of capitals of the columns, embodies the same constructional principles, but in actual fact it was the first and greatest of these, the Doric, that was employed almost exclusively during the great period of Greek civilization and which really merits the name of Greek architecture.

At first sight it seems that nothing could be easier than the correct marshalling of these rows of simple columns and it is only when one understands how large a part illusion plays, how many of these seemingly straight lines are actually curved, that one realizes what a miraculous sense of proportion, how formidable a knowledge of mathematics and what centuries of practice and experiment have been involved in the achievement of this final impression of inspired simplicity.

Curiously enough, the intellectual mastery of the Greeks was quite unmatched by their practical ability. The structural methods employed in building the Parthenon showed little or no advance on those in use in the early Bronze Age, and owing to their inability to discover mortar, the Greeks continued to secure their building blocks by cumbrous and expensive iron clamps right up to Hellenistic times.

THE taste of the Romans, like that of so many Empire builders, tended towards the flamboyant, and it was not surprising therefore that they should have had the temerity to try to improve on the architecture of the Greeks. That this attempt was crowned with but indifferent success is still less remarkable, in that the Greeks had brought their own type of building to so complete a state of perfection that no further development along those particular lines was possible. However, the Romans introduced several remarkable innovations, of which the most daring was the adaptation of the Orders to the construction of buildings of two stories, by superimposing one row of columns on the top of another ; a constructional device that was to provide the basis of much of the architecture of the Renaissance. Another device for the popularization, if not the discovery, of which the Romans were responsible was the round arch, which they used in conjunction with the column to form an arcade.

It is not surprising that it should have been the Corinthian, the last and flashiest of the three Greek Orders, which the Romans used most frequently, nor that in their efforts to outdo the Greeks they should have been led to concentrate on an extreme richness of decoration, which must, one imagines, have rendered Rome in all its glory a trifle overpowering. Augustus, we are told, found the city brick and left it marble, but several of the recent changes in London do not encourage one to believe that such a metamorphosis is necessarily a change for the better.

However, when the Romans forgot for a moment to outdo the Greeks and busied themselves with works such as aqueducts, roads and fortifications, which we should consider to belong to the province of the engineer, they revealed their real genius for construction, and produced monuments that entitle their architecture to a consideration no less serious than that universally accorded to the Greek.

THERE was one feat of construction that the Romans with all their engineering ability had never been able, any more than the Greeks, to achieve. They were perfectly capable of putting a dome on a circular building, but the difficulty of covering a rectangular edifice with this type of roof had always defeated them. The final solution of this problem was reserved for the architects of Byzantium ; that is, the satisfactory solution, for a method of raising a dome on squinches (reducing the square to be covered to an approximate circle by placing beams across the corners) had been practised in the East for centuries ; but the development of the true dome, one resting on pendentives (see p. 189), was Byzantium's great contribution to Western architecture. In the case of England it was a gift which was not applied until centuries later, and by the time that St. Paul's had arisen the dome had been developed and exploited by several generations of Italian and French architects. Nevertheless the credit belongs in the first instance to the Byzantines.

The very success with which the problem of the dome had been solved had an inhibiting effect. So perfect was the solution arrived at that no modification or extension of the original plan was possible ; whereas the Gothic cathedral remained throughout the Middle Ages a living organism expanding and developing with the adoption of new techniques, the Byzantine church remained always in a state of suspended animation.

Although Santa Sophia ranks with St. Peter's and Chartres as one of the three great masterpieces of Christian art, Byzantine architecture has exercised little influence on that of western Europe, and until Westminster Cathedral was built no architect had the courage to attempt to revive it on a large scale.

THE earliest mode of building employed in England was one in which everything, including shelter, was sacrificed to obtain an effect of rugged grandeur. Simple in design, the principal buildings in this style nevertheless presented a series of exceedingly tricky problems of construction, and the labour and ingenuity required to manœuvre the vast monoliths into position must have been considerable. The successful achievement of such feats (without the assistance of any cranes and machinery) indicates the existence, even in that remote age, of that spirit of dogged perseverance and tenacity which has done so much to make British architecture what it is to-day. Incidentally it is interesting to note that even then British architects were actuated by a profound faith, which has never subsequently wavered, in the doctrine that the best architecture is that which involves the most trouble.

The actual date of such erections as that represented on the opposite page has never been accurately determined ; the building in the left foreground, however, can with some degree of confidence be assigned to the second or third decade of the twentieth century A.D.

THE earliest style of medieval architecture in Western Europe is known as Romanesque, save in England, where, for patriotic reasons, it is always referred to as Norman. It was an admirable, straight-forward method of building—what the French call " une architecture franche "—with none of those sleight-of-hand tricks that for some people render the later Gothic styles so disturbing, and flourished until the close of the twelfth century. The enormous pillars quite obviously support the roof and together with the immensely thick walls give the spectator a welcome feeling of security. One never receives the impression that a Norman church has by some curious natural process sprung up out of the ground ; the first glance is sufficient to assure one that its construction has cost a great many people a great deal of very hard work. Owing to the simplicity of their construction almost all the examples in this style achieve a dignity and a repose which is frequently lacking in later buildings whose more complicated and scientific structural methods have presented the builders with greater opportunities for exercising their imagination.

For the amateur the Norman style possesses another great advantage ; of all the medieval styles it is far the easiest to recognize. Once you have assured yourself that the arches are round not pointed, you are in a position to pronounce with conviction that it is a Norman building at which you are looking. And in nine cases out of ten you will be right, for luckily Mr. Ruskin and the other nineteenth-century revivalists did not consider Norman a sufficiently fancy style to merit revival for ecclesiastical purposes, and in England its use in modern times has been confined almost exclusively to railway tunnels. In Germany, however, where of course it was known as Romanesque, it was regarded more favourably, and several very fine barracks and even one or two churches were built in this style, and in America it aroused the enthusiasm of several nineteenth-century architects of whom the most notable was perhaps H. H. Richardson.

IT used once to be the fashion, when discussing the domestic architecture of the Normans, to stress, with a certain degree of high-minded relish, the considerable sacrifice of comfort in the interests of security. " Those vast walls, three foot thick, those slits of windows, that damp unhealthy moat, what a fearful testimony they provide," a previous generation of social historians were wont to exclaim, " of the unappeasable bellicosity of our rude forefathers ! " To-day, while still agreeing wholeheartedly with these conclusions, those whose memories of life in England during 1940–41 are still vivid find it less easy to maintain that happy note of cultured superiority.

Nevertheless it remains perfectly true that the Normans were forced by the prevailing insecurity to live in small isolated communities protected, from the irredentist tendencies of the Anglo-Saxon peasantry and the too easily aroused enmity of their fellow barons, by outworks and bastions the size and thickness of which inevitably reduced the living space. Thus in the majority of castles there was one communal living-room and one only, the Great Hall, in which the lord and his higher retainers lived, ate, and slept. In a few of the more elaborate examples there were one or two sleeping apartments hollowed out of the thickness of the wall for the ladies of the household. In all cases, however, the lower servants slept in the stables.

However intolerable such a state of affairs may seem to us, given the conditions of the eleventh century, this architecture was purely functional. And, moreover, in at least one case it retains its function in the twentieth, for the presence of a large castle in the centre of one of the principal cities of Wales, retained and treasured for antiquarian reasons, was acknowledged during the late war to have saved the town council large sums in the provision of air raid shelters.

D URING the Middle Ages the original Spartan simplicity of the Norman home suffered progressive modification, and if no very high degree of comfort was finally attained, at the end of the period the houses of the rich compared very favourably with, say, the average first-class waiting-room in a modern provincial railway station.

In the course of time increasing security from internal disturbance led to the gradual abandonment of all but the most modest fortifications—a carp-stocked moat and a few token battlements—so that it was possible to increase both the number and size of the rooms. Nevertheless the hall retained its old importance and the majority of the household continued to spend most of their time beneath its now rather more elaborate and considerably larger roof.

A taste for privacy, however, was beginning to emerge, and in the wealthier homes the master and mistress, and occasionally their children, had small bedrooms of their own and there was frequently a parlour, called a solar, in which the ladies of the house were accustomed to occupy themselves between meals. At the same time the upper classes began to interest themselves in the question of decoration and the plain white-washed walls of their Norman ancestors were hidden behind tapestries, painted canvas or frescoes according to the financial resources of the house-holder. In most houses the hall was still heated by means of a brazier in the middle of the room, the smoke from which was optimistically assumed to disappear through a hole in the ceiling, and it was not until the very end of the Middle Ages that the fireplace and chimney became anything like general, even among the well-to-do. Needless to say when this novelty first appeared it was roundly attacked by the conservative on moral grounds ; the comparative absence of smoke secured by this new device was bitterly regretted by all those, and they were as numerous then as now, who clung to the old English belief that if a thing is unpleasant it is automatically good for you. An immediate and shameful weakening in the moral fibre of the nation was confidently predicted.

Apart from these few improvements the home life of the period was much the same as it had been in Norman times. Glass was still very rare and the wooden lattices, which appeared at this date, let in considerably more wind than light and the floor was covered with rushes which were changed at the most infrequent intervals,—an unhappy arrangement since, as in all English country houses at every period, there were far too many dogs.

LATE in the late twelfth century some anonymous genius discovered a new method of vaulting whereby the masonry of the roof was supported by a series of stone ribs, and the whole body of architects, fired by the spirit of competition, set to and in very short time evolved a number of ingenious improvements. Hitherto, a very large number of pillars and immensely thick walls had been necessary, but now it was discovered that by means of a judicious disposition of buttresses and the new system of vaulting used in conjunction with the pointed arch, the weight could be more evenly distributed and a greater proportion of wall-space devoted to windows. Although it is sometimes maintained that the credit for this revolutionary discovery belongs to an anonymous Englishman, it cannot be denied that the French made far better use of it and that the Early English style produced no single building in any way comparable with Chartres. At the same time there developed an enormous enthusiasm for decoration which found its chief outlet in covering the capitals of the pillars, the surrounds of the doors and windows and in fact every available space with a riot of intricate carving, producing an effect which (in the case of most of the English examples) it must be confessed was ingenious rather than beautiful.

Another notable feature of the style were the west fronts of the cathedrals and larger churches, which were covered from top to bottom with sculptured figures arranged in rows of niches, representing the most notable figures of the Old and New Testaments and a large selection of saints. It is customary to refer to these façades as " the poor man's Bible "—a custom which prompts the reflection that the poor Man of the Middle Ages must have enjoyed quite exceptional eyesight. In the hands of a master, as at Peterborough, the effect can be overwhelmingly beautiful, but it was a device that needed very careful handling and none but the most pig-headed medievalist can sincerely maintain that the west front of Salisbury, for instance, is an unqualified success.

DECORATED

AT the beginning of the fourteenth century Gothic building underwent a further change, and the resulting style is frequently known as Decorated (for reasons that remain a trifle obscure in that in most cases, the decoration, though invariably rich, is not noticeably more conspicuous than in either of the other two styles of Gothic architecture). The most notable development which distinguished this new style from Early English was in the windows. Formerly these had been of narrow lancet shape, and when a large window was required at the east end or at the termination of the transepts, this could be obtained only by grouping three lancets together with the tallest in the centre. With improved methods of construction it was now found possible to build thinner walls, and so the divisions between the lancets were reduced to two thin shafts terminating in elaborate tracery of curvilinear design. Alongside this elaboration in the treatment of the windows there occurred a corresponding development in the construction of the pillars. Already in Early English churches the pillar had been enriched by the addition of subsidiary shafts tacked on to the sides supporting the vaulting ; now it vanishes completely and its place is taken by a sheaf of slender columns of equal size.

Of the three styles of Gothic architecture in England it is the Decorated that has been the most frequently undervalued. The virtuosity and breath-taking qualities of Perpendicular and Ruskin's powerful championship of the simple virtues of Early English have both tended to overshadow its less obvious beauties. Moreover, with the exception of Exeter it is not a style that is worthily represented in our cathedrals. But nevertheless, some may consider it the greatest of the three, for in the finest examples (the parish churches of East Anglia, for instance) there is evidence of a mastery over materials to which the Early English architects never attained and which the Perpendicular architects frequently abused.

PERPENDICULAR

UNLIKE the other three styles of medieval architecture, which were common to all northern Europe, Perpendicular was a purely English discovery and its masterpieces cannot be paralleled anywhere abroad. This style, which attained to its fullest development in the second half of the fifteenth century, was the logical outcome of a curious passion for height, operating within the conventions of the Decorated style of the previous age. All the elements of the latter style are still here but curiously distorted and changed ; the vertical lines have become fantastically prolonged and when at last they curve inwards they do so far more abruptly, giving to the resulting arch a curiously flattened form. In addition, a number of horizontal bars appear in the tracery of the windows, rendered essential by the need to provide some support for the thin perpendicular shafts. At the same time the system of vaulting grew ever more complex and it became customary to indulge in a superabundance of ribs and bosses, the majority of which fulfilled no structural purpose, until finally the system known as " fan-vaulting " was evolved ; an architectural device which arouses enormous enthusiasm on account of the difficulties it has all too obviously involved. Externally the most remarkable features of the style were the flying buttresses, which although they occur in other methods of building, are here developed to a most fantastic pitch of ingenuity. It is as though the Perpendicular architect abhorred any unnecessary expanse of masonry and was desirous of eliminating every square inch of solid stone that was not absolutely essential to the stability of the building ; even battlements which were still retained round the roof for decorative purposes were pierced and hollowed until they resembled nothing so much as a plan or map of themselves. Many of the most notable examples of the style differ from vast conservatories only in that the framework is of stone, not iron or wood and that the glass is coloured.

It must nevertheless be admitted that the admiration evoked by the more extravagant examples of the style is not always unqualified by a faint distrust aroused by the " Look !—No hands " attitude of which they would seem on occasion to be the expression.

DURING the Middle Ages the science of architecture had seldom been applied to domestic building save in the most rudimentary fashion. It was the Church which had cultivated and developed architecture, as it had the other arts, and applied it to the erection of cathedrals, churches and monasteries. Of the laity far the largest class, the agricultural labourers, lived in primitive cottages built of mud (as they still were in certain parts of the country, notably Devonshire, until quite recently) ; the burghers, although latterly often in a position to spend time and money on the decoration of their houses, were prevented by the cramped conditions of the walled town from indulging in any elaborate architectural experiments ; the nobility, up to the very end of the period, were interested only in those aspects of the science which dealt with fortification. Even so vast and celebrated a building as the royal palace of Clarendon seems to have been little but an enormous collection of halls and small rooms, all on one level, added to and enlarged as convenience and the whims of various monarchs dictated, enclosed by a moat and wall, and presenting hardly any features of strictly architectural interest.

But with the firm establishment of the Tudors conditions altered and the country gentry had now the leisure and the necessary assurance of safety to turn their minds to the development of the unfortified manor house. The actual appearance of such houses differed widely from district to district ; in some parts the presence of quarries near at hand enabled the builder to work in stone, elsewhere he was forced to be content with timber and plaster, or in certain districts, brick. The actual form of the house was dictated by the material, but the plan in every case remained in its essentials medieval, for although the country no longer suffered from constant civil wars the memories of past dangers were still vivid and led to the retention of many of the features of the castle.

THE coming of the Tudors coincided with the beginnings of the Renaissance, but not for a long time was visible in England any thing more than the first faint flicker of the dawn that in Italy had already ended the long nightmare of the Middle Ages. Thus the Tudor home in its fittings and furniture was only a rather more elaborate version of that inhabited by the previous three generations. The timber-work supporting the roof became ever more complex but the construction remained the same in principle ; tapestry shared the honour of being the most fashionable wall-covering with carved panelling ; and although carpets were imported from the East in larger numbers, they were still used as table coverings and wall decorations and never as carpets. However, the number of rooms increased rapidly and although the Great Hall still retained its importance, it tended to be reserved for meals and ceremonial occasions instead of being used as the general living-room for the whole household day in and day out. But towards the end of the period political events were the indirect cause of a considerable alteration in the generally accepted plan of a gentleman's mansion.

When Henry VIII dissolved the monasteries he presented their buildings to those whom he considered the most deserving of his friends and who thereupon set about converting them into country seats. Now throughout the Middle Ages the standard of comfort and convenience in the religious establishments, with the exception perhaps of such strict orders as the Carthusians who had never abandoned their original austerity, had been far higher than that prevailing in even the most palatial private house ; moreover, the number and size of the principal rooms was, of course, far greater. The result was that the English nobility and gentry suddenly acquired a taste for size and grandeur in their residences that they never subsequently lost.

However, it must be admitted that in the process of conversion the average monastery lost much of its original comfort and practically all its convenience, but the desire for such things remained and flourished, and enlightened persons such as Erasmus started bitterly to complain about the general untidiness, beastliness and smelliness of the average English home.

THE parallel between the age of Queen Victoria and that of Queen Elizabeth I has provoked frequent comment and explanation. Both, it is frequently pointed out, were ages of expansion and both made imperishable contributions to our national literature. But as far as architecture and decoration are concerned the background against which Shakespeare lived and worked was hardly more attractive than that which displayed Alfred Lord Tennyson to such advantage.

In the arts, the age of Elizabeth was one of transition ; the old medieval restraints had been abandoned, but nothing as yet had appeared to take their place, so that the architects with a number of new processes at their disposal were at a complete loss as how best to apply them. As a result houses increased enormously in size but not in beauty. The comparative cheapness of glass led to a sudden enlargement of the windows, that had hitherto been extremely small, producing an effect that called forth the comment that such houses were " more glass than wall." Vague rumours of what was happening in Italy together with a sudden flood of cheap and ill-drawn pattern books containing what the artists hoped were classical details encouraged architects to embellish the gaunt and still fortress-like mansions of the nobility with a fiendish variety of pilasters and cornices of the proper meaning and application of which they were totally unaware. The tremendous literary enthusiasm of the period invaded architecture and led to the introduction of numerous mottoes as decorative features which appeared in every available position, both inside and out.

In certain districts, notably Gloucestershire, a pleasant and unpretentious style of domestic architecture was evolved which so long as it remained unaffected by foreign influences produced buildings of much merit and charm. Needless to say when, late in the nineteenth century, an Elizabethan revival took place, it was the flashiest and most grandiose specimens that were taken as models.

QUEEN ELIZABETH'S grandfather was Lord Mayor of London and the immediate ancestry of the majority of her nobility was, from the point of view of the College of Heralds, even less memorable. In fact the Elizabethans were, almost to a man, *nouveaux riches* ; and in the decoration of their homes they employed all those symbols of recently acquired culture with a heartiness and an abandon which, when displayed by more recent generations, have seldom failed to provoke the polite merriment of the cultured readers of *Punch.* The typical figure of that golden age was not, it is sobering to reflect, the dashing cloak-flinging figure of historical fiction, but none other than our old friend Sir Georgeous Midas.

In the home the immediate effect of this change-over in the seats of the mighty was to produce an atmosphere of oppressive and overwhelming richness. The comparative simple linen-fold panelling of Tudor times gave way to acres of woodwork carved and chiselled with patterns of quite staggering complication and hideousness ; no sooner had a more plentiful supply of glass led to the installation of larger and more numerous windows than a rich gloom was at once brought back by the practice of filling every window-pane with dubious heraldry ; and although new methods of construction rendered unnecessary the presence of those pendant nodules so beloved of the builders of fan-vaults and hammer-beam roofs, their place was promptly taken by clusters of disturbing and quite unnecessary plaster stalactites. Decoration for decoration's sake was the motto of the Elizabethans and every available inch of wall, ceiling and furniture was covered with lozenges, strap-work, heraldry and all the as yet completely undigested classical bric-à-brac of the Italian Renaissance.

However, in one respect at least the period marked an advance. Although the decoration of the Elizabethan house was in no way an improvement on that of the previous generation, the plan was markedly superior. The Great Hall while retaining its central position loses much of its former importance and at meal-times the family now abandon its draughty wastes to the steward and upper servants in favour of the cosier if less impressive winter-parlour. Moreover, the appearance of a grand staircase in addition to one or two of the old circular variety renders the first floor both more accessible and more popular, and it is at once further enriched by the presence of a long gallery, an impressive apartment used for exercise on wet days and the display of numerous paintings of well-dressed but frequently mythical ancestors.

NO great change of style marks the division between the reigns of Elizabeth and her cousin James, and in the realm of interior decoration the passage of time is only indicated by a progressive and welcome simplification. The new nobility were slowly becoming accustomed to their rôle and were no longer so conscious of the need to mark their transition into the ranks of the upper classes by an overwhelming display of real wealth and bogus heraldry. As a result the average Jacobean interior is not, save in the region of the fireplace, quite so oppressively a background against which the contemporary woodcarver and plasterer can display unhindered their grisly talents. Moreover, although the average local builder's understanding of the four orders and other elements of classical architecture, which he acquired from cheap text-books translated from the Italian, remained shaky in the extreme, there is evidence of a growing mastery. The proportions are still almost invariably wrong but they are not quite so wrong as they had been formerly.

However, if no very drastic change is to be detected in the decoration of the house itself in the matter of furniture, the Jacobeans displayed a praiseworthy spirit of invention. Hitherto the well-dressed man had always worn well-padded breeches attaining, in the last years of Queen Elizabeth's reign, quite staggering dimensions ; now suddenly these went out of fashion and for the first time he was in a position to appreciate the painful disadvantages of the plain wooden chair. As a result the stuffing was now transferred from the sitter's backside to the chair he sat on, and upholstered furniture was introduced for the first time to a grateful public. Needless to say such luxuries were confined to the very rich, and for many years to come the less sensitive bottoms of the lower orders continued to rest on hard wood.

The style loosely described as Jacobean remained popular, with slight modifications, until the Restoration, but nevertheless as early as the reign of James the direction in which English domestic architecture was logically to develop had been firmly indicated. When Inigo Jones built the Queen's house at Greenwich the Middle Ages were brought to an end and the English Renaissance, which was to find its highest expression in the architecture, decoration and furnishing of the home, had begun.

D

RENAISSANCE

WHILE in England men were busy raising those fantastic ecclesiastical conservatories in the Perpendicular style of Gothic architecture, in Italy architects were already busily engaged on the first and greatest of revivals. Why the ruins of ancient Rome, which had been visible for centuries, should suddenly have attracted attention at this particular moment in time is a question to which the reader will find no answer here. However, whatever the reason may have been, it was a highly welcome development, for the Gothic style was finished. After the Perpendicular, and kindred styles abroad, no further development was possible and the latest examples exhibit many of the signs of complete spiritual exhaustion.

In classifying Renaissance architecture as a revival one is perhaps guilty of a misstatement, for while Greece and Rome supplied both the inspiration and the architectural motifs of the style, and although Renaissance architects all paid homage to Vitruvius and boasted of the accuracy with which they followed his precepts, in practice they never hesitated to abandon them whenever their fancy dictated, and thus their buildings may be said to represent a development and an extension of the classic tradition rather than a slavish resuscitation of a long-lost method of building. For a long time England had little or no share in this new movement, and until the seventeenth century the only signs that a fundamental change had taken place in architectural theory and practice were a few inexpertly copied capitals and pilasters tacked on to the fabric of houses which remained resolutely medieval in plan and construction. Although long delayed, the English Renaissance was destined to have a truly splendid flowering, and in fact this time-lag may be said to have been an advantage, for when English architects first became acquainted with Italian architecture, it was already an established style with many different schools and variations, and they could view it with a thoroughness and a detachment that would have been impossible at the time of its enthusiastic inception.

THE first Renaissance style to be introduced into England was the Palladian, so-called after Palladio who had developed it in north Italy in the sixteenth century, and Inigo Jones was its principal, in fact, almost its only, exponent. But in the second half of the seventeenth century there emerged the figure of the second of our great English architects, and one of the greatest architects of all time, Sir Christopher Wren, who although he had no first-hand acquaintance with the architecture of Italy, evolved from it a style less rigid than the Palladian, of a greater richness and one that was completely suited to the English climate and character.

The greatest achievements of this style were St. Paul's Cathedral, and the innumerable city churches built by Wren and his pupils after the Great Fire. Here one is at a loss to know what to admire most ; the seemingly endless variety of treatment and invention which achieves the miracle of avoiding all suspicion of sameness and monotony in half a hundred different churches all erected within a few years of each other ; the restraint of the handling coupled with the largeness of the conception which prevents grandeur from declining into the merely grandiose ; or the incredible skill and ingenuity with which so, at first sight, intractably Gothic a feature as the church spire (a form which the English medieval builder had developed with conspicuous success and one which therefore possessed a national significance) was preserved and reinterpreted in classical terms, although quite unknown to antiquity.

In one respect only did the builders of these masterpieces fail ; they not infrequently chose sites which the churchmen of a later age considered might be sold for much money and given, if not to the poor, at least to the Ecclesiastical Commissioners.

ON THIS SITE WILL
BE ERECTED THE
MAGNIFICENT
NEW PREMISES
OF THE
PHOSGENE
DEVELOPMENT Co

WHEN the Pilgrim Fathers first alighted on the inhospitable shores of New England it was hardly to be expected that their intention to start a new way of life would at once find expression in a new architecture. The immediate problem was the provision of shelter, and any observable stylistic innovations are the result of the practical adaptation of familiar models to withstand new conditions rather than the outcome of an intense preoccupation with architectural theory. The basic design which the settlers brought with them was that evolved in the south-eastern counties of England during the course of the sixteenth and seventeenth centuries. The high-pitched roof (due originally perhaps to Flemish influence, always strong in East Anglia) was admirably suited to the heavier snowfall of the American winter, and construction in wood, the only readily available building material, presented no problems to ships' carpenters from coastal towns long familiar with the technique of weather-boarding (or clap-boarding as in America it has come to be called). In the course of time as the colonists became better adjusted to their environment various ·modifications were introduced. Thus the overhang, a useful device in the crowded conditions of town life for gaining extra floor space on the upper storey, which was found to serve no practical purpose where space was no object, was gradually abandoned, and the projecting gable that was a highly developed feature of contemporary building in the old world proved unsatisfactory in the new, owing to the annual accumulation of snow in the angles which tended after a time to rot the supporting woodwork.

By the beginning of the eighteenth century all the necessary adjustments had been made and with the introduction of the sash window a few years later the basic American small house was fully developed. So satisfactory did it prove that it has remained fundamentally unchanged ever since and seems likely, anyhow in the New England states, successfully to survive the challenge of the open-plan split-level.

WITH the return of Charles II to his kingdom there opened a period which, decoratively speaking, lasted until the middle of the nineteenth century. A period in which continuous changes and improvements took place, but changes and improvements that developed naturally and progressively one from another and were the result of no sudden break with tradition. During the Commonwealth, England had enjoyed a state of almost complete artistic stagnation, but in the person of Sir Christopher Wren there arose an architect whose interior design was no less ingenious and satisfying than the steeples of his city churches. Moreover, the long exile abroad of the King and court led to the introduction of foreign, particularly French, modes, and fashion becomes of almost equal importance with convenience in the arrangement of the home. Now for the first time there appears upon the scene the smart and mondaine figure of the interior decorator.

The Great Fire of London made possible the speedy development of the town house proper ; hitherto it had been for the rich merely a country mansion which chanced to be in a town and for the middle classes a conglomeration of rooms over a shop jutting ever farther into the street. Now the genius of Wren devised a plan for London houses which, in essentials, remained unchanged until the coming of the flat. At street level a small entrance hall, a dining-room and a parlour ; on the first floor a large state room and principal bedroom ; above more bedrooms and closets and below ground that rather unfortunate device, the basement kitchen, that had been introduced from Italy at the end of the sixteenth century. The beauty of this plan lay in the fact that it could be modified or enlarged to suit almost all pockets and every variety of site.

The interior walls are still covered with panelling but the panels themselves are of good proportions and fewer in number ; moreover the exasperating gap between the ceiling and the woodwork is now banished and the cornice appears in the proper place. Monotony is avoided by the employment of richly carved mouldings and all that jungle of inefficient woodcarving is replaced by a few festoons of very naturalistic fruit, confined usually to the fireplace and the panels immediately above it. The whole effect is, perhaps, rather heavy but at least it is a well-proportioned heaviness.

LOUIS XIV

ALTHOUGH the *Grande Monarque* was by no means alone among his royal namesakes in lending his name and number to a style of decoration, he at least bore a considerable amount of the responsibility for the style so called. The great palace of Versailles was the fruit of his own inspiration and every inch of the decoration bore in some degree the impress of his personality, and, as Versailles was immediately copied in every country in Europe and continued to provide the model for the perfect palace so long as palaces continued to be built, he can perhaps claim to have had as much influence in interior decoration as any other single individual. For although very few people are actually called upon to live in palaces, a very large number are unwilling to admit the fact, and so a style devised for the further glory of a seventeenth-century French monarch has been eagerly adopted from time to time not only by other royalties great and small but also by English noblemen, Jewish businessmen, South African diamond kings, American millionaires and film-stars of all nations.

In England during the seventeenth century there was on the whole too little money to encourage the accumulation of those vast mirror-bedecked, satin-hung, generously gilded suites of enormous rooms, but in one respect the example of the builder of Versailles was eagerly followed with direct results in the sphere of interior decoration. The habit of receiving in bed, so popular with both sexes among the very wealthy and important, led to that apartment being decorated with uncommon luxury and pomp. The walls beneath a heavily gilded and carved cornice were hung with damask of a colour and pattern to correspond with the bed curtains. The ceiling, divided into variously shaped panels by heavy mouldings, was prettily enlivened with a variety of cleverly painted rapes ; and the general interest of the apartment was still further increased by a liberal supply of pictures, Susannah and the Elders, Samson and Delilah, Judith with the head of Holofernes and other such subjects, in which a certain popular appeal was judiciously balanced by the warrant of Holy Scripture.

THE characteristic that distinguished the Renaissance from all other revivalist movements, both architectural and religious, was its almost inexhaustible vitality. After the first rush of enthusiasm it did not peter out and die ; the vital creative force behind it continued to function for close on four hundred years, constantly discovering new forms of expression while still employing the same classical idiom. It was as though an ingenious small boy was bent on discovering how many different buildings he could put up with the same box of bricks. Half-way through the seventeenth century, however, it appeared as though every possible combination had been exhausted, whereupon the small boy, not in the least deterred, proceeded to use his bricks as counters in a dazzling display of juggling.

This ability to employ architectural forms for purposes for which they had never been intended—in order to express movement or obtain an effect of drama—and get away with it, was the whole secret of Baroque. Vast flights of steps, innumerable statues, elaborate fountains were all pressed into service for the sake of a truly impressive effect, to obtain which the Baroque architect did not hesitate to twist columns until they looked like sticks of barley sugar, cover cornices in rich folds of imitation drapery, extend façades until they were twice the height of the buildings they masked, and finally, if time or money ran out, to paint whole vistas of staircases and colonnades he was unable to achieve three-dimensionally. That it was a highly dangerous proceeding, which could be justified only by complete success and called for an almost incredible degree of virtuosity on the part of the architect, was proved by the unhappy efforts to revive it made in England at the beginning of the present century (see Edwardian Baroque).

It is not therefore surprising that with the exception of Vanbrugh and Hawksmoor, no English architect of that period was encouraged to try his hand at the Baroque, for cleverness is a quality that, in architecture no less than in life, we have always been notorious for regarding with ill-concealed dislike.

ATASTE for the grandiose, like a taste for morphia, is, once it has been fully acquired, difficult to keep within limits, and all the various potentates who during the first decades of the eighteenth century so eagerly followed where Louis XIV had led, soon found themselves provided with residences which, while being undoubtedly of an extreme impressiveness, fulfilled just about as many of the ordinary requirements of a home as do the Pyramids. Seldom have architects achieved dwellings further removed from the definition of a house as *une machine à habiter* than such masterpieces as Wurzburg, the Winter Palace, Zabern and Blenheim. Ceilings only incidentally fulfilled their usual rôle of covering a room ; their primary purpose was now to provide a background for the athletic amours of Jupiter and other inhabitants of Olympus cleverly and lovingly depicted by Tiepolo, Lebrun or Verrio. Pillars and columns might possibly support an arch or cornice but were just as likely to be employed for their decorative value alone. Staircases no longer took the shortest route from one floor to another but writhed and curled in every direction—vast processional ways designed for the passage of half the Almanach de Gotha in full war-paint —and every inch of available wall-space was covered with trophies, busts, caryatids and escutcheons in marble, malachite, gilt, plaster, and shell-work.

This state of affairs could not, of course, last for long. Few of his fellow-sovereigns enjoyed the robust health of the Sun King and the enormous discomfort of living in these glittering barracks, which not all the ingenuity of science nor all the wealth of the Indies could warm, and in which the dining-room might be anything from a hundred yards to a quarter of a mile from the kitchens, soon drove them to build smaller, though scarcely less luxurious, residences in the parks attached to their main palaces. But nevertheless this passing passion for pomp and glory at all costs was not without its effect on the art of decoration. The main staircase then acquired an importance which it never subsequently lost, and the taste for long vanishing vistas of columns and arches led to the introduction of the *trompe l'œil* whereby the desired effect could be obtained at a quarter the cost and which retained its popularity as a method of wall decoration for many years to come. Above all, the decorative artist then acquired a freedom and an increased power of invention without which the rococo style of the next generation could never have been devised.

THE style of domestic architecture illustrated on the opposite page is frequently referred to as Queen Anne, although few monarchs have displayed less interest in architecture than that sovereign ; nor was its practice confined to her reign. It would be both more rational and more just to call it Wren, for it was first brought to a state of perfection by that great man and further developed and popularized by his immediate followers. It was the first fully developed style of domestic architecture to be employed in England. Here the cornice, pilaster and other motifs borrowed at second-hand from classical antiquity have become completely assimilated and, used in conjunction with brick, form the foundation of a great national tradition.

Although it is customary to regard the numerous country houses and palaces as the great masterpieces of the style, Wren and his followers may perhaps be considered even more worthy of praise for their triumphs in urban architecture, for it was their peculiar merit to have devised, at a time when the whole capital had to be rebuilt after the Great Fire, a type of house that was not only completely satisfactory in itself, but one which could always be employed as a unit in a larger scheme. They did their duty not only by the householder but also by the street. And the fact that their example was followed by all the various schools of architecture that flourished throughout the eighteenth century, and was only neglected in the nineteenth, is responsible for much of whatever architectural merit London as a city may still be thought to possess.

E

WHEN the prosperity of the Southern States reached the point where the plantation-owners could relax and think about gracious living, the most popular model for a gentleman's residence in the Old Country was that evolved by Wren and illustrated on page 49. It is not surprising, therefore, that this admirable achievement should have provided the earliest model for the American country mansion, but it is strange that it should have retained its popularity over so long a period. As late as the first decade of the nineteenth century houses were still being built, wide eaves, projecting cornice and all, particularly by the wealthy ship-owners of Rhode Island and Massachusetts, in a style which was beginning to look old-fashioned in England in the reign of George I. Although both the Palladianism of Lord Burlington and the influence of Adam are frequently reflected in the interior decoration of eighteenth-century American homes, they have left but scant traces on the façades. Only the widespread use of the Venetian (or Palladian, as in America it is more correctly called) window beloved of Wyatt testifies to any awareness overseas of what, in the mid-century, was going on at home.

Naturally enough, while the earliest examples are almost indistinguishable from their English prototypes, in the course of time various modifications dictated by local conditions were generally adopted. Thus the invariable presence of shutters rendered necessary by the hotter summers lends a faintly Gallic air to many an uncompromisingly Anglo-Saxon façade, and an understandable reluctance to have the slaves' quarters too near the house, accounts for the absence of those flanking wings, which for those accustomed to the lay-out of English houses of a similar grandeur, so imposing a central block would seem, on occasion, to demand.

Although the original English plan was in most cases strictly adhered to, the materials in which it was carried out are often different. Stone is almost non-existent and wood frequently replaces brick. However, the claim so constantly made by proud owners, for whom English brick has come to have almost the same social significance as has the dovecote for the proprietors of French *manoirs*, that all *their* bricks were imported from England as ballast should be treated with reserve. America, even in the seventeenth century, was not wholly devoid of either clay or kilns, and if but half these stories are true, it is necessary to visualize a quantity of ballast crossing the Atlantic every season throughout the eighteenth century sufficient, at a rough calculation, to sink the *Queen Mary* twice over.

THE great triumph of the architects and decorators of the Rococo period was the discovery of a way to reconcile the demands of fashion and comfort. The invention, skill and virtuosity of their predecessors of the Baroque have seldom been surpassed but, as has already been pointed out, their masterpieces rarely achieved that indefinable air of cosiness, of being *chez soi*, a desire for which must from time to time assail all but the most robust megalomaniacs. Now there was developed a style of decoration in which most of the familiar motives of baroque reappear but are treated with a lightness and a freedom which renders them admirably suited for the decoration of apartments conceived on a less heroic scale. The old division of the wall into panels is retained but the lines of the mouldings lose their former stiffness and are broken into curves, or garlanded with flowers or terminate in elaborate scrolls or shell-work. Chairs, mirrors, picture-frames—all lose their old arbitrary shapes, and the cornice over a door may dissolve before one's eyes into a mountainous oriental landscape, or a pediment blossom forth into a bundle of corn tied up with ribbons. Obviously this could become unbearably tiresome and boring, but such was the sureness of taste of the masters of this style, so consummate their control of their material, that in nine cases out of ten such pitfalls were widely avoided.

It would, however, be a mistake to assume that Rococo was a hard and fast style which only flourished for one short period ; it is far rather a way of feeling, a mood which may recur in any sufficiently sophisticated epoch. After its popularity had declined on the continent it suddenly reappears once more in England and produces the Brighton Pavilion. During the Victorian era it vanishes from sight (although it left its mark in the decoration of those *papier-mâché* and mother-of-pearl trays and boxes so popular in the early years of that reign) only to re-emerge again at the very end of the century and find a deplorable expression in *Art Nouveau*. But never has it achieved such triumphs as it did in the mid-eighteenth century, when its sudden blossoming coincided with the maturity of such master craftsmen as Pöppelman, Cuvillies and Chippendale.

THE expansion of London and the increase, both in numbers and importance, of the middle-class, provided the eighteenth-century architect with one of his most important tasks. The problem of housing large numbers of city merchants and professional men, all with big families, at no great distance from their place of business, at the same time maintaining some order and dignity in the process of extending the city, was not a light one, but nevertheless the solution arrived at was, granted the social conditions of the time, as nearly perfect as possible and constitutes one of the great triumphs of English architecture. This happy result was largely brought about by the development in combination of the two great discoveries of contemporary town planning—the terrace and the square. The first presented the architect with a unit sufficiently large to allow him to achieve impressive and dignified effects which his descendant, who is forced to manipulate a row of detached houses designed for clients clamouring for something different in a pathetic effort to assert an individuality they do not, in fact, possess, can never hope to emulate to-day. The second preserved sufficient of the country in the shape of grass and trees to form an agreeable contrast with the surrounding bricks and mortar and sufficient light, air and space to render it pleasant and healthy and to facilitate the movement of traffic.

The resulting style was not confined to England but spread to America, where its most notable remaining monuments are to be found perhaps in the neighbourhood of Boston Common.

To-day we are busy pulling down these districts as quickly as possible on the grounds that the houses are difficult to run, which may be true, and sneering at them on the grounds that they are monotonous, which certainly is not. By means of such simple devices as the recessed arch, the decorated fanlight and the sculptured keystone, the eighteenth-century architect avoided monotony with a skill and a subtlety which seems always to elude the designers of the pseudo-American cliff-dwellings of Park Lane. For the boredom occasioned by too much restraint is always preferable to that produced by an uncontrolled enthusiasm for a pointless variety.

IN England comparatively few homes, and those only of the very rich and smart, reflected even faintly the glitter of the baroque and rococo fireworks sent up by the contemporary continental designers. The average English room during the first half of the century was simply a logical development of the Restoration apartment evolved by Wren and his followers. As time went on the mouldings and cornices became lighter and the introduction of new woods, such as mahogany, produced a greater variety of panelling, but the chief advance was displayed not so much in the decoration of the room itself but in the furniture it contained. Formerly this had been very restricted in quantity and almost standardized in design, but now an innumerable supply of objects began to accumulate in various corners, owing their introduction not to their utility but solely to their decorative value. An ever-increasing supply of porcelain, coming at first from the Far East and later from the factories at Bow and Chelsea, invaded the mantelpiece and eventually demanded special glass-fronted cupboards for its accommodation and display. Niches had to be made to shelter the busts of Roman worthies which the antiquarian enthusiasm of Lord Burlington and the Dilettanti unearthed from the soil of Italy in suspiciously large quantities. And the tireless industry of Augustan poets and High Church divines rendered the presence of numerous large book-cases essential for the proper equipment of a gentleman's home.

These innovations were for the most part the reflection of the master's taste and sensibility, but along with them others that indicated feminine influence were now introduced into the decorative field. While panelling, painted or plain, remained the most popular form of wall covering in such masculine apartments as the library and dining-room, in the bedrooms and boudoir its place was being taken by wall-papers, usually imported from China, and silk and satin hangings.

Moreover, there was one field in which the rococo spirit proved as fertile in invention in this country as in France or Germany—that of Chinoiserie. The china and paper coming in large quantities from the East proved a powerful source of inspiration to our designers and from now until almost the end of the century there flowed a constant stream of furniture, plasterwork and painted panelling all of which embodied Chinese motifs, and in the treatment of which contemporary craftsmen, above all Chippendale, displayed a taste and invention in no way inferior to those which found expression in the pavilions of Potsdam and Nymphenburg.

IN the second quarter of the eighteenth century there arose among English intellectuals an extreme enthusiasm for Italy and things Italian, and a young man's education was considered incomplete if he had not visited that country. Very soon in all the arts, but more particularly music and architecture, it became *de rigueur* slavishly to copy Italian models. As a result the popularity of the Palladian style, that had first been introduced nearly a century earlier by Inigo Jones, enjoyed a new lease of life, and one enthusiastic and noble amateur even went so far as to erect on the banks of the Thames a house that was a model of a villa that Palladio had built on the banks of the Brenta.

At first sight it might be thought that this new Palladian revival would have had a stultifying and unhealthy effect on English architecture, but happily such was not the case, for the English architect, if sometimes a little lacking in originality, has always displayed a remarkable skill at adaptation (unfortunately he has not always been endowed with a correspondingly developed ability to exercise his judgement in respect to the models he adapts), and it was not long before the style had become completely acclimatized.

About the middle of the century it was further modified by a renewed interest in antiquity, which led to a further adaptation, this time, however, at first hand, of motifs from Greek architecture. It might be thought that a style to the formation of which so many diverse elements had gone— Palladian, Wren, Palladian again, Greek Revival—and which paid such attention to various academic formulae, would have been unlikely to produce many masterpieces. Whereas, in fact, whatever buildings may be thought to entitle English architecture to a place alongside that of the other countries of Western Europe, were almost all produced in the period which started after the Great Fire and ended on the death of George III. Which just shows that in architecture it is the architect, not the formula, which counts.

THE changes in public worship brought about by the Reformation of religion presented ecclesiastical architects in all Protestant countries with some interesting problems. But in England the position was more difficult than elsewhere owing to the strictly limited (though curiously ill-defined) nature of the religious transformation. The emphasis on the word of God expounded at considerable length by a powerful preacher not only switched the focus from the altar to the pulpit but necessitated a large increase in the seating accommodation, for not even the most devout congregation could be expected to stand throughout the normal seventeenth-century sermon. For the Calvinist the solution was comparatively simple, a plan which enabled the maximum number of people to hear the Scriptures expounded with the maximum force, but for the Anglican, a member of a communion which still proclaimed itself Catholic and remained sacramentally minded, the difficulties were considerable, and, in fact, no generally accepted answer has yet been found.

But if the ideal plan was never achieved the problem of adornment was forcefully and immediately solved by the simple device of almost total suppression. Anything which could conceivably be considered as giving rise to idolatry was taboo, and it was surprising how many things could. Salvation might easily be imperilled by a cross on a prayer-book, and a candle in the wrong place was assuredly a beacon on the path to perdition. Fortunately the Renaissance provided architects with a range of detail and ornament to which, at least for those who had never visited Southern Europe, no possible hint of Popery attached.

In England itself, complete and unmodified examples of the typical church interior finally evolved by the genius of Wren, Gibbs and their followers are few, for all the more important specimens bear fearful witness to the misguided enthusiasm of the Tractarians. Windows designed for clear glass glow with raw sienna and crimson lake ; classical vistas are broken by neo-Gothic rood-screens ; Carolean woodwork is concealed by Anglo-Catholic frontals. But across the Atlantic, where in the nineteenth century the supply of churches was still way behind the demand, such Ritualists as flourished were far too busy building new places of worship to attempt to modify existing ones, even if, which in the religious climate of the United States was unlikely, they had been given the chance. As a result anyone seriously interested in the development of Anglican church architecture in the eighteenth century must make the pilgrimage to America where the tradition of Wren and, more particularly, of Gibbs, found its fullest expression and is most perfectly preserved.

THE main, in fact the only, influence in English architecture from the seventeenth century onwards had been classic ; Italian classic with Inigo Jones, French and Dutch classic with Wren and his followers, Italian once more with Lord Burlington and Kent. Now another foreign fashion arises, still classic, but totally different from the foregoing modes. This time it is the decorative art of antiquity itself, as revealed by the excavations at Herculaneum and later Pompeii, that brightens the walls and ceilings of Mayfair. This development might quite easily have ended in disaster, for the whole movement was surrounded with a vast amount of donnish pedantry and expertise ; moreover, the taste of ancient Rome as displayed at Pompeii is strongly suggestive of Tottenham Court Road ; but fortunately at that moment there arose a new generation of architects and designers, headed by the brothers Adam, whose genius enabled them to take this unpromising material and evolve from it a style which remains one of the greatest glories of the applied arts in this country.

With enormous skill the urns, sphinxes, vine leaves and all the rest of the boring bric-à-brac of the first century of our era are now moulded in plaster, ormolu and other materials, painted, gilded and rearranged on candelabra and mirrors, on friezes and cornices in such a way as to achieve the most varied yet homogeneous scheme of decoration. At the same time panelling disappears from the walls which are painted in plain flat colours with narrow bands of moulding outlining plain areas of varying shapes but invariably excellent proportions. Great attention is lavished on the ceiling on which ovals and lunettes painted with antique scenes by the talented Miss Kauffman are surrounded by an elaborate geometrical tracery of gilded plaster. On the floor, as like as not, is a specially woven carpet reproducing the pattern overhead. Over the doors entablatures and cornices of an impeccable correctness support busts and urns while the blank spaces on the walls are enlivened by medallions.

It is at this time that the supremacy of the interior decorator is finally asserted. Hitherto this profession, developed if not invented by Kent, had, while not being altogether unlucrative, scarcely attained the dimensions of a full-time job. Now the brothers Adam (incidentally far better decorators than architects) established it firmly on that smart and fashionable plane on which to-day so many bright young men and shrewd old women so profitably operate.

TOWARDS the end of the eighteenth century there was noticeable in almost every sphere of human activity a growing craving for Romance. In architecture this nostalgia was particularly marked and took the form of a polite enthusiasm for the styles of far away and long ago. Chinese, Indian, Egyptian and Gothic methods of building all in turn enjoyed a remarkable vogue among the *cognoscenti*, but it was the last style that proved most popular and the revival of which was to prove, though not at once, most disastrous for English architecture. So long as the traditions and conventions governing the thought and manners of the eighteenth century remained in force, all was well. The patrons of architecture were enlightened and well-educated men who were perfectly aware that a wholesale revival of Gothic methods of building would be intolerable, but regarded, quite rightly, the building of a cottage or two in what they hoped was a medieval but were quite certain was a picturesque style, as perfectly permissible. Thus the gazebos, the *cottages ornés* and the summer-houses which formed the principal output of the Gothic architects of the period, bore little relation to any known Gothic style ; they remained, in fact, perfectly ordinary eighteenth-century cottages on to which had been tacked a row of castellations and a couple of plaster gargoyles. Ninety per cent of these productions had little connection with architecture at all but were simply the work of smart interior decorators trying their hand at landscape gardening, or literary amateurs of exhibitionist tendencies creating a suitable background for their carefully cultivated personalities. Nevertheless, out of this innocuous and rather charming chrysalis would one day come blundering the humourless moth of Victorian revivalism.

AT the beginning of the nineteenth century the rapid rate of London's expansion was still further accelerated, and it was the great merit of the architects of the day, of whom the most memorable though not the most gifted was Nash, that they realized that if chaos was to be averted, all future developments must be considered not as isolated streets and districts but as part of one rational and carefully considered plan. If the numerous new squares and crescents that were then put up all over London, but more particularly in the north-west, were not the equal of the best work of the previous generation, it was largely the result of the speed with which they were erected that led to the sacrifice of detail for the sake of a fine general effect.   It is this preoccupation with the total mass that gives to the best Regency architecture its impressive vistas and slight but not unwelcome theatrical air.

But while the greatest triumphs of the style were gained in the design and lay-out of large terraces, it proved almost equally successful when applied on a smaller scale.   The numerous villas erected at this time both in London and along the coast—incidentally no one has ever devised a style of building that harmonized better with the scenery and atmosphere of the English seaside—with their delicate ironwork balconies, their ingenious and successful bow windows, and their coats of sensible and attractive stucco, are among the most charming and original small buildings in the whole history of English architecture.

THE artistic enthusiasm of the polite world having once been directed towards antiquity showed no signs of abating. Rather did it become more intense with time and tended to concentrate on ever earlier phases of civilization. Thus the Pompeian was soon superseded in the popular favour by the Etruscan, which in its turn was swept aside by the Greek, which last maintained its sway unchallenged save by the Egyptian, for a brief period immediately following Napoleon's eastern campaign, for close on half a century.

This new passion for antiquity reached its highest pitch in France where it became indissolubly connected first with the French Revolution and secondly with Napoleon. It is therefore the first example which history affords us of an ideological style ; that is to say a style adopted not so much for its own beauty or convenience but rather for the sake of the political qualities of the civilization that first evolved it. Certainly no style had ever proved so all-embracing. Architecture, furniture, painting, women's dress, military uniforms all approximated as closely as possible to what were piously hoped to be antique models. Luckily, however, very little Greek furniture had survived the centuries so that designers were forced to use their own imagination and that soulless mechanical copying which is the bane of all revivals was very largely avoided.

In England that robust national common sense, which had not yet been sapped by the Romantic movement, saved us from the more ridiculous excesses of *le style Empire* and a very pleasant and serviceable style of decoration was evolved in which these new neo-Greek fantasies were skilfully grafted on to the old, trustworthy eighteenth-century stem. At the same time the exuberant and artistically dominating character of the Regent himself led to a more lavish display of gilding and more dashing use of colour. Formerly blues and greens in pastel shades were most commonly employed but now such assertive tints as terra-cotta and maroon spread themselves over the walls, while for curtains and upholstery sulphur yellow, royal blue and crimson generously sown with wreaths, stars, cornucopias, lyres and sphinxes were used with the most resolute self-confidence. Full-blooded yet intellectual, aristocratic and at the same time slightly vulgar, the Regency style was sufficiently paradoxical to be perfectly in tune with the age which gave it birth and to lend some shred of justification to its popularity to-day.

DURING the last quarter of the eighteenth century the writings of Winckelmann, the excavations at Pompeii and the rediscovery of the Doric temples in Sicily and Southern Italy combined to produce a world-wide enthusiasm for the styles of classical antiquity, more particularly the Greek. While no country of western Europe remained wholly unaffected by the resultant Classical Revival in architecture, the most numerous masterpieces of the style are to be found elsewhere. In both Russia and America, and for not wholly dissimilar reasons, the years following 1812 were a period of expansion and saw a considerable increase in building activity, and in both countries a style in which the most spectacular effects could be achieved comparatively easily in wood enjoyed an understandable popularity.

In the recently united States the task of adapting the old eighteenth-century plan to the requirements of the new style did not, anyhow in the sphere of domestic architecture, present many difficulties. The introduction of a frieze, usually Doric, beneath the cornice, the imposition of pediments, straight or triangular, above the windows, an increased emphasis on the portico, already a well-established feature which now became the principal element in the design of the façade, and the job was done. Moreover, the resulting composition proved easily and unexpectedly adaptable to a number of requirements besides the purely domestic. Surmount the roof with a tower and lantern and you had a church ; replace the lunette in the pediment by a gilded eagle in low relief and you achieved a state-house ; while the simple device of inscribing one's name in bold Egyptian type along the frieze immediately transformed a stately mansion into the most impressive and confidence-inspiring of banks. Widespread throughout the States, the Classical Revival has, thanks to the careful researches of so many film producers, come chiefly to be identified with the South, for as every student of the cinema knows it is unthinkable that any Southern belle worth her salt should wave good-bye to the boys in grey, riding away between the moss-hung ilexes while the mocking-bird calls from the magnolia, save from a Doric portico, and no properly brought-up planter's family would dream of assembling to hear the news of Gettysburg from a wounded trooper in any but the severest neo-Greek setting. And the producer's insistence on Classical Revival is fully justified not only on stylistic but also on economic grounds, for the next time he comes to shoot *War and Peace* the sets can, with perfect architectural propriety, be used all over again with no additional expense except for the snow.

THE terrace house, which in England had proved so satisfactory a solution to the problem of urban accommodation in large centres of population, was not called for in America during the eighteenth and early nineteenth centuries where the pressure on living-space was not so great, and few examples are to be found outside such comparatively large towns as Philadelphia and Boston. Nevertheless, when in many Southern cities a demand arose among the local territorial magnates for a town residence it proved impossible even in those expansive conditions simply to line the streets with full-scale replicas of their country mansions. The compromise arrived at was both ingenious and aesthetically pleasing. The main block of the country house was set at right angles to the street and the portico, which had previously been in the centre of the façade, was expanded to cover what was now the side of the house and provided with a screen wall at ground level pierced by the front door. Not only did this enable the town-planner to accommodate a far larger number of houses in a given space but the provision of a *piazza*,[1] catching any breath of wind, ensured a through draught as well as a relatively cool living-place, in the heat of summer.

This simple but effective arrangement, first developed in Charleston at the end of the eighteenth century, proved so satisfactory that it continued to be employed in brick, wood and stone with but slight alterations of a purely decorative nature right up to the outbreak of the war between the States. Moreover, not even the substitution in the nineteenth century of wrought iron for wood in the construction of the *piazza* disturbed the harmony for, particularly in New Orleans, this feature was thereupon carried to an extraordinary point of elaboration and fantasy with the happiest results.

---

[1] The history of this name is not, perhaps, without a certain interest. When in the seventeenth century the first formal square on the continental model came to be laid out in London it was called, not unreasonably, the Covent Garden Piazza. The feature of this innovation which principally struck contemporaries was the provision of covered arcades on all four sides, and in the course of time, as this novelty was eagerly copied, the usage of *piazza* for any open arcade became general, and was applied by the colonists to the wide porticoes which in a hot climate they soon found to be an agreeable convenience as well as architecturally chic.

THE average American householder, anyhow on the Eastern sea-board, is extremely fortunate in that his forebears, constrained by the practical limitations imposed on all pioneers, evolved a straight-forward, workaday dwelling-house which for several generations the restraint and sobriety encouraged by their religious faith forbade them to embellish. When early in the nineteenth century the cheap machine-made nail made possible the development of the " balloon frame," the standard home developed from the seventeenth-century settlers' house could be mass-produced with the minimum of alteration and adjustment and before long a very large proportion of the total population of the United States were living in white-painted frame houses that differed from those of their ancestors only by the addition of a porch and, perhaps, a " monitor " roof.

It can be argued that seen *en masse*, or without the sheltering elms with which so many of them are happily surrounded, the effect is not invariably of the most stimulating interest, but few who are familiar with the com-muters' paradises of England, enriched with stained glass door-panels, horse-shoe porches, half-timbering, pebbledash and what-have-you, are likely to condemn the temperamental passion for conformity which dis-courages the average American from attempting that personal touch with which so many British home-lovers seek unsuccessfully to distinguish their own particular semi-detached castle from all the others on the by-pass.

"IN these years" (1850–1870), as Mr. Guedalla informs us, "a noble impulse among architects was covering England with reproductions of the medieval antique, of which the Law Courts are the stateliest, the Randolph Hotel at Oxford not the least worthy example." By the middle of the nineteenth century the Gothic Revival had ceased to be a joke ; the driving force behind it had changed from fashionable whimsy to an evangelical (the word is used in no narrow denominational sense) fervour. The Gothic was now regarded not merely as the most beautiful method of building but also the most True ; a practical demonstration of the permanent validity of Keats' celebrated definition of æsthetic worth. It was a shrewd move on the part of the poet to inform us, albeit rather tartly, that the interchangeability of Truth and Beauty " is all we need to know," for despite the gallant efforts of Mr. Ruskin, embodied in a score of thick volumes, the precise reason why any one style of building should be truer than another remains impenetrably obscure.

The revivalists, however, were not burdened with overmuch intellectual curiosity, and taking the poet at his word forged ahead, creating for posterity a noble legacy of schools, town halls and railway termini all in the purest style of the thirteenth and fourteenth centuries. At first they had confined themselves largely to ecclesiastical buildings, but had soon come to the conclusion that what was good enough for God was good enough for Cæsar and in less than no time half the public buildings in the country were enriched by a splendid abundance of crockets and gargoyles, *meurtrières* and encaustic tiling.

To a lay observer it might seem that one of the principal objections to the revival of the Gothic style lay in the fact that it had evolved under conditions which found no parallel in the modern world, but in practice this objection was found to be invalid. Indeed, its greatest merit in the eyes of the architect of the period lay in its splendid adaptability, and when Sir Gilbert Scott's plan for a Gothic Foreign Office had to be abandoned owing to the unenlightened attitude of Lord Palmerston he was able by a few strokes of the pen to transform it into St. Pancras Railway Station.

WHILE the more ambitious nineteenth-century manifestations of the Gothic spirit in architecture may, with very few exceptions, be dismissed as deplorable, certain of the minor achievements still retain a vague period charm. In particular some of the smaller country railway stations represent a most unexpectedly successful outcome of a brave, but admittedly uncalled-for, attempt to adapt the methods of building, popular in ecclesiastical circles in the fourteenth century, to the needs of the machine age. Their merits, it must be admitted, have very little connection with architecture, but nevertheless they frequently achieve an air of cosy whimsicality not out of keeping with the spirit of our British Railways. Moreover, it cannot be denied that up till the present none of the Railway Companies (with the honourable exception of London Transport) have evolved a style for this particular type of building that is not equally inconvenient and twice as offensive.

Another branch of architecture in which this unpretentious form of Gothicism operated, with, alas, considerably less success, was the erection of public conveniences. These necessary and useful reminders of the limitations of humanity present a difficult problem for the architect ; no one wishes that they shall be overwhelmingly conspicuous, but on the other hand they would belie their name were they too cunningly concealed.

The Gothic revivalists' gallant attempt to combine modesty with prominence by erecting small-scale models of fourteenth-century baptisteries in cast-iron and equipping them with the necessary plumbing was not, however, a solution to the problem that entitles them to any praise save on the score of ingenuity.

THE slightly frivolous enthusiasm for Gothic modes, which had in Georgian times resulted in so many charming and tasteful additions to the parks of the nobility and gentry, fortunately survived undimmed although operating at maximum voltage only on a slightly lower social plane, when the educated response to Gothic had been purged and transformed by Victorian zeal. Villas in St. John's Wood and cottages at Ventnor continued to flaunt their barge-boards and their lancets until well past the middle of the century, when the middle classes finally succumbed to the purer and more austere appeal of North Oxford. But across the Atlantic, unreproved by Ruskin and undiscouraged by Sir Gilbert Scott, this Biedermeyer mediævalism, which flourished from the 'forties onwards, achieved, thanks largely to fortunate timing, masterpieces of an elaboration and a fantasy unequalled in its country of origin.

By great good fortune the United States first awoke to the beauties of the Revival just at the moment when improved tools, such as the fretsaw, and an increase of pattern-books had inspired all the more ambitious carpenters with an unbounded self-confidence. Urged on by some unknown Horace Greeley saying " Go Gothic, young man, go Gothic ! " these pioneers responded with enthusiasm, and it was not long before a casual visitor might be forgiven for thinking that all the cuckoo clocks in Switzerland had been set down on the banks of the Hudson.

Ridiculous, but never without charm, at the furthest possible remove from *machines à habiter*, these *cottages ornés* mark an important stage in the history of the United States. They were the product of a civilization that was at last in a position to evolve for itself a luxury style that paid little or no regard to purely practical considerations. Carpenters' Gothic is the Rococo of America ; short-lived indeed, but only because with too rapidly accumulating wealth a time soon came when the unpretentious was no longer admissible.

ALTHOUGH the Gothic Revival was making rapid headway through-out the early years of Queen Victoria's reign it did not attain to its greatest popularity until the 'sixties and 'seventies, and while an ever-increasing number of churches and town halls were erected in that style, domestic architecture remained for a long time unaffected. Thus when the great expansion of London during the 'forties and 'fifties led to the development of Belgravia, Paddington and Kensington, the terraces and squares which were erected in these districts were built in a style which, despite a certain monotony and, according to modern standards, consider-able inconvenience, did nevertheless represent the last expiring flicker of the great classic tradition of English architecture. Although the detail was usually inferior to that of the best Regency work and the remarkable inventiveness of that style was lacking, Kensington Italianate at its best, e.g. Eaton Square, did achieve dignity and even a certain magnificence. And even when, as has happened in North Kensington and elsewhere, whole streets and terraces intended for prosperous stockbrokers have sunk to the slum-level, they still retain some faint atmosphere of shabby grandeur. (The ability to survive drastic social reverses forms an acid test for architec-ture and one which it can be confidently said that the arterial housing estates, the slums of the future, will certainly not be capable of satisfying.)

However, despite the impressive effect of the façades, houses built in the Kensington Italianate possessed numerous defects, such as airless and pitch-dark basements and far too many and too steep stairs. In addition, in order to create the full architectural effect intended by the builder it is necessary that all the houses in a block or terrace should receive a coat of stucco of the same colour and at the same time ; a condition which the sturdy individualism of the average British householder has always rendered impossible of fulfilment. Nevertheless, their total disappearance, which seems to be merely a matter of time, will deprive London of much of its character, which the luxury flats and cosy little maisonnettes in Architectural Association Georgian, which are already taking their place in Paddington, will do nothing to restore.

OLD BROWNSTONE

THE conservative impulse which in London led the big speculative
builders to adopt Kensington Classic as the style most suitable for
housing the prosperous *bourgeoisie* operated in the United States,
more particularly in New York, to produce the stylistically very similar Old
Brownstone.   If that which the two styles have in common is at first sight
more apparent than their differences, there are, none the less, some curious
deviations in most of the American variants.

The detail is generally much heavier, attributable no doubt in part to the
change of material, but it is difficult to think of any structural explanation
for the extraordinary overdevelopment of the cornice.   Nevertheless, it is
to these enormous projections supported on those whacking great consoles
that the style owes much of its effectiveness, particularly when employed
over a large area in wide thoroughfares such as Second and Third Avenues.
To attribute the greater height of the basement to any compassionate preoccupation with the welfare of the domestic staff, unshared by his Victorian
counterpart, would be to credit the New York householder with a social
conscience for which strangely little evidence is available.   Having regard
to the racial composition of the population at that time it would seem
more likely that the raised ground floor, common all over Dublin although
practically unknown in contemporary England, was due to Irish influence.
Totally without charm the style does not lack a certain dignity ; sufficiently
pronounced in some cases almost to overcome the affront to the façade
offered by the inevitable fire-escape.

Curiously enough this heavy and not overstimulating style would seem
strongly to encourage the homicidal urge, for, as every keen student of
American detective fiction knows, there is hardly one of these mansions in
all New York that has not witnessed the rubbing-out of an eccentric dowager,
or heard the unseasonable death rattle of a miserly millionaire.

T HE early Victorian or, as some purists prefer to call it, the Adelaide style, while it undoubtedly marks a decline (the elegance of the Georgian and the vitality of the Regency have both departed), nevertheless represents not unworthily the last phase of a great tradition. The lines are heavier, the decoration coarser, yet the proportions are still good and there is a general atmosphere of solidity and comfort. Painted walls now vanish, not to reappear for nearly a century, beneath a variety of patterned papers, striped, spotted and flowered. Mahogany reigns almost supreme as the popular wood for furniture, though both birch and rosewood maintain a certain vogue. Carpets are either elaborately floral in pink and white or severely patterned in billiard-cloth green or scarlet. Fireplaces are comparatively plain in marble.

However, it is not so much the quality of the individual furnishings that has altered but the quantity. Now for the first time the part tends to become more important than the whole and the room assumes the function of a museum of *objets d'art*. The mantelpiece is transformed into a parade ground for the perpetual marshalling of rows of Bristol glass candlesticks, Sèvres vases, Bohemian lustres around the glass-protected focal point of a massively allegorical clock. For the better display of whole cavalry divisions of plunging bronze equestrians, Covent Gardens of wax fruit, bales of Berlin woolwork, the drawing-room, the library and the boudoir are forced to accommodate innumerable cupboards, consoles and occasional tables. The large family portrait loses none of its popularity but the fashion for miniatures and silhouettes enables the range of visible reminders of the importance of family ties to be extended to the third and fourth generation of uncles, aunts and cousins of every degree.

Futile as such generalizations invariably are, one may perhaps hazard a suggestion that nothing so markedly distinguished the average Victorian from other generations as this passion for tangible evidence of past emotions ; a longing to recapture in some concrete form the pleasure of a visit to Carlsbad or Margate, the unbearable poignancy of Aunt Sophia's death-bed. Hence the unbounded popularity of the memento, the *Reiseandenken*, and the keepsake. Harmless and rather touching as such a fashion may be, the intrusion of this aggressively personal note into decoration led to future trouble when it became necessary to find without fail a prominent place for such a surrealist variety of objects as a sand-filled paper-weight from Alum Bay, a lock of little Willy's hair and dear Fido, stuffed and mounted.

SALUBRIOUS DWELLINGS FOR THE
INDUSTRIOUS ARTISAN

"Oh earth the God of Wealth was made
Sole patron of the building Trade."

Swift.

WHILE the Victorian architects were busy erecting tasteful reproductions of Chartres cathedral and the belfry of Bruges (so useful
for factory chimneys) and covering the rather inefficiently drained
marshes on the outskirts of Westminster with the stucco palaces of the
nobility and gentry, it must not be imagined that the needs of the humbler
classes of the community were in any way overlooked. In all the great
new towns of the Midlands and the Industrial North large housing estates
sprang up on which, by the exercise of remarkable forethought and
ingenuity, so great was the anxiety lest the worker should be too far removed
from the sights and sounds of the factory or mine which was the scene of
his cheerful labour, a quite fantastic number of working families were accom-
modated. In order that the inhabitants might have the privilege of contemplating, almost ceaselessly, the visible tokens of nineteenth century
man's final triumph over nature, many of these estates were carefully built
alongside the permanent way, or even, if there was a viaduct handy, actually
underneath it. That the humble householders might recall the country
villages from which so many of them had come, the streets were considerably
left unpaved and the drainage system was made to conform to the primitive
rustic models to which they were accustomed. It is true that it was found
impossible to avoid a certain monotony but this was counteracted by carefully refraining from doing anything to interfere with the effects of the
elements, and allowing the weather full opportunity to produce a fascinating
variety of surface texture.

IN the earlier part of the nineteenth century it was assumed, and rightly, that a little healthy vulgarity and full-blooded ostentation were not out of place in the architecture and decoration of a public-house, and it was during this period that the tradition governing the appearance of the English pub was evolved. While the main body of the building conformed to the rules governing South Kensington Italianate, it was always enlivened by the addition of a number of decorative adjuncts which, though similar in general form, displayed an endless and fascinating variety of treatment. Of these the most important was the plate-glass window which took up a large section of the façade, and was invariably made the excuse for a virtuoso display of decorative engraving in which may frequently be detected the ingenuous working of a native taste for the Baroque that nowadays can only find expression in the decoration of merry-go-rounds and cigar-boxes. Hardly less important were the enormous lantern which was suspended from an equally imposing and lavishly decorated curlicue at the corner of the building, the whole forming a triumph of nineteenth-century ironwork, and the splendid and elaborate examples of the sign-writer's art with which the façade was always generously enlivened.

But, alas, with the spread of popular education even the brewers became cultured and the typical pub, such as the one illustrated here, gave way to every variety of Gothic hostelry and its homely façade was soon hidden behind a copious enrichment of coloured brickwork and encaustic tiles. Says Ruskin sadly, writing in 1872, " there is scarcely a public-house near the Crystal Palace but sells its gin-and-bitters under pseudo-Venetian capitals copied from the church of the Madonna of Health or of Miracles."

But worse was still to come. Half-baked culture was succeeded by a poisonous refinement which found expression in olde worlde half-timbering and a general atmosphere of cottagey cheeriness. Fortunately a number of the old-fashioned pubs still survive in the less fashionable quarters, but the majority of them are doubtless doomed and will shortly be replaced by tasteful erections in the By-Pass Elizabethan or Brewers' Georgian styles.

LE STYLE ROTHSCHILD

" Little bits of porcelain,
Little sticks of Boule
Harmonize with Venuses
Of the Flemish school."

Financier's Song (mid-nineteenth century).

THE Victorian passion for symbols, so essentially charming and domestic in its origins, soon proved capable of considerable expansion. If room could be found for an endless collection of objects whose sole justification was sentimental, then there was ample accommodation available for concrete reminders, not of happy moments of the householder's past, but of the satisfactory state of his financial present. *Objets d'art et de vertu* had been collected by rich men since the beginning of the seventeenth century, but, in the majority of cases, for their own sake ; now they are feverishly sought after for the kudos they acquire for their owners and as visible evidence of enormous wealth. In order properly to display these hoards of Dutch pictures, Italian marbles, German glass and what-have-you, a style was evolved which combined all the richest elements of those which had preceded it and which soon became standardized throughout Europe. The heavy golden cornices, the damask hung walls, the fringed and tasselled curtains of Genoese velvet, the marble and the parquet were as rich and as inevitable in the wealthiest circles of Vienna as they were in London, and formed almost the official background for the flashy pageant of the Second Empire.

Nothing in this style, which we have named Rothschild after what was, until recently, its finest existing example in this country—the old Rothschild house in Piccadilly—was new save the gasoliers : and the only original element was a fondness for the recent past which displayed itself in a taste for the more lavishly gilded examples of Louis Quinze furniture (hitherto each succeeding generation had surveyed the styles of its predecessors with the utmost distaste and when Empire furniture came in Chippendale went out to join the Sheraton and the Queen Anne in the servants' hall). Nevertheless, despite this ample evidence of cultural insufficiency, one is forced to admit, if like Henry James one " can stand a lot of gilt," that it was a style that at least possessed the courage of its opulent convictions. As such it flourished exceedingly on the other side of the Atlantic where it was ideally attuned to the rugged individualism of the age of the Robber Barons.

WHILE the drawing-room, boudoir and bedroom of the average Victorian house might from time to time undergo the most extraordinary metamorphoses, the dining-room retained almost unaltered the character it had acquired at the very beginning of the period until, in many cases, the war of 1914. It seems as though the Victorians while willing to tolerate frivolous decorative experiments in those less important apartments were not for one moment prepared to allow any light-hearted tampering with a shrine sacred to the important processes of mastication and digestion. Moreover, not only was the dining-room safe from purely temporal changes but also from those arising from personal idiosyncrasies so that its form and decoration were practically standardized throughout the upper and middle classes.

The table, sideboard and chairs were invariably of mahogany and of a sufficiently massive construction safely to support the respective weights of the serried rows of decanters and side dishes, the monumental *épergnes* and the diners themselves. The wall-paper was always dark and nine times out of ten of a self-patterned crimson design ; that colour being considered, quite rightly, as stimulating to the appetite. The carpet was invariably a fine Turkey.

Conventions no less rigid governed the choice of pictures. These, if they were not ancestral portraits, had either to be still-lives or landscapes and in both cases the choice of subject was sternly restricted. If they were still-lives they must be those vast pyramids of foodstuffs in which the red of the lobster strikes so bold a note of colour, beloved of the Dutch School ; if landscapes, then storms at sea, Highland cattle or forests of a fearful gloom. (The only permissible exceptions to this depressing range were scenes in the Holy Land and then only if depicted at sunset.) Late in the period conversation pieces were allowed provided the personnel were carousing Cardinals. Generally speaking the only alternative to oil-paintings as a form of wall decoration were steel engravings, preferably by Mons. Doré, of sacred subjects. (It should never be forgotten that the dining-room of the period had taken over some of the functions of a private chapel in that it was invariably the scene of family prayers.)

So lasting were these traditions that the childhood memories of many still comparatively young retain their ineffaceable impress. Thus the sight of a Van der Velde seascape still brings the taste of mulligatawny whistling up from the author's subconscious while the flavour of Bordeaux pigeon summons with all the completeness of Proust's tea-soaked madeleine an unforgettable cloud of Mons. Doré's angels hovering over the Colosseum.

94

"WHATEVER may be said in favour of the Victorians," remarks Mr. P. G. Wodehouse, "it is pretty generally admitted that few of them were to be trusted within reach of a trowel and a pile of bricks." The sage when he made this profound observation was thinking of the English country house of the period ; had he been referring to a similar building of the same date north of the Border it is probable that he would have expressed himself even more forcibly. For awe-inspiring as were the results of the archæological enthusiasm and light-hearted fantasy of Victorian architects working in England, these worthies seem frequently to have reserved the most ambitious efforts of their breath-taking virtuosity for the benefit of their Scottish patrons.

In a praiseworthy attempt to provide the Northern kingdom with an ample supply of stately homes, they evolved a style which they hoped adequately symbolized the rugged virtues and lurking romance of the inhabitants of

> Caledonia stern and wild
> Meet nurse for a poetic child

and which they christened Scottish Baronial. It was, as the name implies, essentially an upper-class style and one which mirrored faithfully that passion on the part of the nobility and gentry for combining the minimum of comfort with the maximum of expense that has always exercised so great an influence over our domestic architecture. Spiral staircases of a steepness and gloom that rendered oubliettes unnecessary ; small windows which made up for the amount of light they kept out by the amount of wind they let in ; drains which conformed to medieval standards with an accuracy which in the rest of the structure remained an eagerly desired but as yet unattained ideal. These were among the invariable features of the style, but were looked on as but a small price to pay for the impressive silhouette, the battlements, the corbels and cloud-piercing turrets of the granite-laden exterior. Moreover, if the Dear Queen could not only endure but actually welcome these little inconveniences inseparable from a truly baronial exist-ence in the Highlands, how could lesser mortals complain if they cracked their skulls on the old-world groining in the Baron's privy or caught pneu-monia from the bracing wind that whistled so romantically through the latticed windows of the brand-new keep ?

Although the Scottish Baronial was primarily a domestic style, it is interesting to note that it was also extensively employed for prisons.

THE official religion of Victorian England is usually considered to have been an evangelical form of Christianity suitably modified to bring it into harmony with a public school education and the principles of free trade, but one is sometimes tempted to wonder whether in large tracts of the country, particularly in Scotland, an older faith that blended ancestor worship with totemism did not reassert its hold on the upper classes from about the 'fifties onwards. How else can we explain the sudden appearance of those vast, castellated barracks faithfully mimicking all the least attractive features of the English home at the most uncomfortable period of its development, and filled with rank upon rank of grimvisaged, elaborately kilted forebears? What other explanation can be found for the presence of these enormous necropolitan menageries stuffed full of stags and caribou, bears and tigers—creatures which, however attractive in life, in death perform no function but the constant employment of legions of housemaids with dusters? What other reason can be advanced for the phenomenal popularity of Mr. Landseer whose only merit as a painter was the tireless accuracy with which he recorded the more revoltingly sentimental aspects of the woollier mammals?

Whether or not Scottish Baronial has its origins in primitive religion its popularity was soon assured in all classes of society. Tartan, stags' heads and faithful representations of Highland cattle in various media soon enlivened the Coburg simplicity of the Court as successfully as they added to the discomfort of cosy little villas in Tulse Hill or Twickenham where the rafters were unlikely ever to ring with the sound of the pipes. And to-day many a dusty hotel lounge, many a dentist's waiting-room with their ritual display of these old symbols, recall, like the mosques of Spain, the former domination of a vanished faith.

AS the name implies, Second Empire Renaissance was a style that had its origins across the Channel, and while over here it never attained to its ripest development we can nevertheless boast sufficient examples to render it worthy of mention. Its most prominent feature, and that which unfortunately seems chiefly to have impressed those who sought to acclimatize it in England, was the Mansard roof. However suitable this device may be on top of the Louvre it altogether fails to produce an effect of inevitable rightness amid the less exalted surroundings of Victoria Station. Unfortunately it had to recommend it the supreme quality of cheapness ; with its aid a whole extra storey could be obtained at a considerable reduction of expense. As a result it has become the almost invariable termination for half the office blocks and luxury flats erected during the last half-century and until quite recently its popularity showed few signs of diminution.

Other notable features of the style were the superabundance of shutters, whose purpose in nine cases out of ten was purely decorative, and at least one pair of ornamental urns suitable for the cultivation of the pinker varieties of geranium. The materials most favoured were yellow and red brick, pointed with great care and very white plaster, and Portland stone, elaborately rusticated, with every variety of slate and fancy leading for the roof. In England the style was generally employed for offices, hotels and railway stations, but one or two examples of its use in domestic architecture do nevertheless exist. They are, however, comparatively restrained in character and lack the staggering richness of such a masterpiece as the Travellers Club in Paris.

WHILE in England Second Empire Renaissance enjoyed but a limited success, being confined almost exclusively to the postal district S.W.1, its popularity in America, particularly in New York State, was phenomenal. As examples multiplied, subtle changes of emphasis and curious distortions became increasingly apparent and very soon a style, of which the original character had been defiantly Gallic, was transformed into one of the most forceful and unmistakable expressions of the nineteenth-century American way of life.

At first sight the difficulties of reinterpreting in wood the highly elaborate motifs of a style which in its country of origin had given so much employment to so many skilled stonemasons, might well have seemed insuperable ; but so to assume would have been grossly to underestimate the invention and resourcefulness of the American carpenter, flushed with triumphs recently gained in coping with the Gothic. In next to no time he was turning out balusters and consoles with all the ease and virtuosity with which so short a while before he had produced ogives and finials. And on these, too, he left the impress of his own personality, thereby endowing the whole style with an unmistakably national character.

To-day these mansions, too frequently in decay, when seen in the autumn dusk, shrouded with hemlocks, with the dead leaves overflowing from the cracked urns and the broken shutter swinging on the rusty hinge, are invested with a strange but genuine poetry. Melancholy symbols of the thwarted hopes of an over-confident generation, their message is akin to that of closed branch-lines and bolted chapels. Too self-conscious to be naïve, insufficiently so to be sophisticated, they yet retain in their decline a dignity with which it seems unlikely that any imaginable change of fortune will invest the ruined split-level or the abandoned motel.

THE peculiar danger inherent in all revivals is the inability to stop. Once a certain style has been revived there is, alas, no reason why one should not go ahead and revive all the others, and this is exactly the fate that overtook nineteenth-century architecture. Having reintroduced the Gothic with such success, the guardians of Victorian taste began seriously to consider whether there might not be some other historic style which had been hitherto overlooked that was more easily adapted to modern requirements than that of the ecclesiastical buildings of the thirteenth and fourteenth centuries. Towards the end of the third decade of the century there developed a suspicious enthusiasm for the architecture in vogue during the reign of a former dear Queen, and the streets of London were soon enlivened by the appearance of numerous buildings in a style that proudly proclaimed itself, on grounds that strike an unbiased observer as being exceedingly slender, as " Queen Anne."

The more remarkable features of this new style were a fondness for very bright brick red, a profusion of enrichments in that most deplorable of materials, terra-cotta, and a passion for breaking the skyline with every variety of gable that the genius of Holland has produced and a good many that it had not. Whole streets in the neighbourhood of Hans Place and Cadogan Gardens were re-erected in this new style and the cultured frequently pointed out, with considerable pride, that the wayfarer in that high-class residential district might easily imagine himself to be in Vermeer's Delft. As time went on, various other features, many of them borrowed from the Arts and Crafts movement of the 'eighties, were incorporated in this style, of which perhaps the most important was a real loathing for symmetry that resulted in numberless bow-windows bulging out in unexpected places and an inability to refrain from employing the most unsuitable materials, such as lead and beaten copper, in an unnecessary attempt to lend variety to an already hopelessly confused façade.

Fortunately many of the masterpieces of this style have survived untouched, and a short bus-ride down Sloane Street will take the student to a district that has hardly changed since the day when Mr. Wilde was called away from it on urgent business.

FROM the beginning of Queen Victoria's reign until the early 'seventies the decorative arts had undergone little modification ; details became slowly coarser, colours ever more garish and after the Great Exhibition of 1851 this process of gradual decline was much accelerated, though there were no signs of any drastic change. But now a variety of strange breezes sprang up from several directions at once which in combination succeeded in blowing the stuffy yet cosy atmosphere of the average Victorian interior to oblivion.

Hitherto the Pre-Raphaelites had been an obscure artistic clique unknown to the majority of the public, but suddenly their practices and doctrines attained a new prominence and soon all the female inhabitants of such artistic neighbourhoods as Chelsea and South Kensington developed a strange, goitrous affliction of the throat and the cheerful magentas and sulphur yellows were banished from their homes in favour of sage green, peacock blue and every variety of ochre. At the same time the fervent mediævalism, that had been flourishing architecturally since the beginning of the century, under the influence of William Morris (the best of whose wallpapers were the only legacy of any artistic value bequeathed us by the whole movement) developed a philosophic-cum-economic tinge which found its final expression in the Arts and Crafts movement. And curiously enough as we have just seen, there sprang up alongside this revived Gothicism a reaction in favour of the classicism of Queen Anne which was responsible for Pont Street, and which led to a hasty dash being made to the attics to rescue whatever had survived in the way of early eighteenth-century furniture.

Unfortunately the contemporary culture had hardly had time to digest these diverse and revolutionary influences when a new and even more disastrous treasure-house of art was discovered in the Far East. Soon the Blessed Damozel was yearning down from between pendant Japanese fans ; the cast-iron mantelpiece, tastefully incised with sunflowers by Mr. Walter Crane, supported two Chinese ginger-jars and a vase of Satsuma ware in which a solitary lily bore witness to the high regard in which the oriental ideals of flower arrangement were now held ; and the Queen Anne furniture, so lately restored to the drawing-room, had to share the honours with chairs and sofas whose spiky frailty was assumed to be oriental in inspiration if not in actual origin. Surrounded by such testimonies to her sensibility as these the intellectual young woman could safely relax and lend a properly appreciative ear to the patter of Pater and whispers of Wilde.

THE cult of æstheticism (some of the effects of which we have considered a few pages back), though flourishing in the 'seventies, was only accepted whole-heartedly by a comparatively small section of the population—the *haute Bohème* of the day. But in the following decade it penetrated in a modified and truncated form into every drawing-room in the land. Needless to say its better features, such as the wall-papers of William Morris and its theoretical insistence on simplicity, never achieved more than a very limited popularity, whereas the blue china, the Japanese gewgaws and the spindly furniture received a rapturous welcome in every home from Tulse Hill to Belsize Park. However, it must not be supposed that the new arrivals dispossessed any of the existing ornaments ; room was found for all and the artistic little snuff-bottle from Yokohama shared a corner of the mantelpiece (now tastefully draped with fringed green plush) with the shell-work light-house from Shanklin.

It was not long before these treasures were joined on their already perilously over-crowded ledges by a new wave of invaders (the whole process is one which inevitably calls to mind the constant penetration of the Picts and the Celts and the Jutes and the Angles and practically dictates the employment of ethnographical jargon) and, by the end of the century, the problem of *lebensraum* had become acute. These newcomers were a tribe of china shepherds and shepherdesses hailing from a strange Kate Greenaway-cum-Marcus Stone conception of the eighteenth century—examples of a now extinct school of plastic art, a few specimens of which are still occasionally to be found, for some inexplicable reason, in the windows of old-fashioned dairies.

But perhaps the most striking feature of the period is the extraordinary love of plant-life which manifests itself in every interior. Aspidistras, palms, rubber-plants and every variety of fern thrive and flourish on all sides, while, no longer living but still decorative, the bull-rush disputes with the pampas grass the possession of the costliest available vase. Dimly through the jungle half-light one perceives on the walls, in very wide gold mounts, the exquisite water-colours of Mr. Birket Foster and many talented studies of irises and other artistic flowers by the young lady of the house. And when the gas is turned up and all the myriad green leaves, swaying in time to the strains of Balfe or of Tosti cast strange shadows on the chrysanthemum-covered wall, one would fancy oneself in some tropical fairyland as yet unpenetrated by the dauntless Doctor Livingstone.

THERE was one type of interior which, although its distribution was always far more limited, rivalled in persistence the Victorian dining-room—namely the masculine apartment known as the study or more familiarly the den, of which many examples are still to be found in schools, colleges, and country vicarages differing hardly at all in furniture and decoration from those in which professors, divines and ecclesiologists laboured and reflected when the Gothic Revival was still young. It was never a style that one would find in every house ; only in the homes of public school men of a studious type. It had as little attraction for Ouida's guardsmen and W. S. Gilbert's æsthetes as it has for their descendants to-day, but nevertheless it may perhaps be thought to represent, as does no other Victorian style, all that was best in that great age. The prevailing atmosphere of high thinking and plain living, of *mens sana in corpore sano*, may be a trifle oppressive, but it is balanced by an undeniable air of comfort.

The details are almost invariably the same and must be familiar to many of my readers—and perhaps painfully so, for when in youth one heard that dread summons " You will come and see me in my study after chapel," it was always to an apartment such as this that one was bidden. The Gothic grate behind its club fender, the groups of long vanished rugger players beside the pipe-rack on the mantelpiece, the Arundel prints in their ecclesiastical mounts hanging between the faded sepia photographs of Greek temples and Swiss mountains, the Gothic book-case with its dusty rows of Paley's Evidences and the brown-backed volumes of the Badminton Library,—all these are changeless and inevitable. Likewise the little marble model of the leaning tower of Pisa, the lump of stone from the Acropolis, the whiskered ecclesiastics in Oxford frames and the large bow window looking on a garden dark with laurels.

To-day such isolated examples as exist represent, like those ruined temples in the jungles of Yucatan that are said still to be tended by some last uncomprehending survivors of the old Maya priesthood, the final dying outposts of a vanished culture. But they can still on occasion arouse a powerful nostalgia in the breasts of all but the most hard-boiled.

AS the old Queen's reign drew to a close, the eighteenth-century note in interior decoration became more marked. In smart circles the thin spindly chairs in shiny black wood, etched with little gold lines that had been so popular in the 'eighties, were gradually replaced by pseudo-Hepplewhite creations in rose-wood and satin-wood. With the arrival of the South African millionaires, the Style Rothschild, which had always proclaimed itself eighteenth century in inspiration, enjoyed a new lease of life and numerous needy cabinet makers and French polishers were kept busy preparing a fresh supply of genuine Louis Seize furniture. At the same time fireplaces ceased to provide a riot of artistic tiling and tended to be " after Adam." And the potters of Dresden found ample employment in the large-scale manufacture of bewigged and hooped figurines, of an archness that the eighteenth century would have found overwhelming.

However, it must not be imagined that this new passion for the styles of Louis Seize et Quinze produced any fundamental change in the appearance of the average drawing-room. The jackdaw strain inherent in every true Victorian, which led to the constant acquisition of innumerable objects of dubious virtue, was stronger than ever, and the crowded ranks of knick-knacks received numerous additions. The new-born consciousness of our Imperial destiny led to an influx of native handiwork from every quarter of the globe—interesting little plaster statuettes of Indian servants, brass trays from Benares, cedar-wood boxes and tables of every size and shape, lavishly inlaid with mother-of-pearl—while an increase in the size of photographs brought innumerable aunts and uncles, dim royalties and dimmer generals from out the decent obscurity of the family album and scattered them in heavy silver frames all over the room. To accommodate all these new-comers, as well as the original inhabitants, the mantelpiece soon proved quite inadequate, and in order to cope with what were rapidly becoming slum conditions that interesting structure the overmantel was devised, which not only served to relieve congestion but also provided an admirable opportunity for the skilled wood-carver to do his ingenious worst.

On the walls the exquisite productions of Lord Leighton and Sir Lawrence Alma Tadema still enjoyed pride of place, and it was not until the very end of the century that a revived interest in the works of Greuze led to their gradual removal, first to the spare room, then to the bathroom landing and finally to the servants' hall.

AT the end of the nineteenth century a certain malaise was discernible in the artistic world : which was not perhaps surprising, for after a prolonged surfeit of Municipal Gothic, Pont Street Dutch, Jubilee Renaissance and other exotic styles it is remarkable that the " O-God-I'm-so-tired-of-it-all " attitude had not been adopted years before. However, until the late 'eighties William Morris, the celebrated inventor of the Simple Life, remained a voice calling in the willow-shrouded wilderness of Kelmscott. Now, however, his teaching bore a sudden crop of exceedingly odd fruit which in course of time came to be christened *Art Nouveau.*

While the hall-mark of this new style was proudly claimed by its supporters to be extreme simplicity coupled with purity of line, honesty compels one to admit that, as one of its spiritual begetters said of truth, it was seldom pure and never simple. Asymmetry, which we noticed as being so popular in the later development of Pont Street Dutch, now became an absolute fetish. Walls staggered inwards from the base, gables shot up at the dizziest angles and doors and windows never by any chance appeared at the points where one was accustomed to find them. While it was originally conceived as a rural style, efforts were soon made to adapt it to urban requirements and rows of quaint and whimsy little cottages, all pebbledash and green shutters, appeared in the northern suburbs of London in clusters which their builders considered themselves justified (by the presence of two sunflowers and a box hedge) in calling Garden Cities. Another interesting fact is that a row of such houses was never called a street but always a Way.

From surroundings such as these did the New Woman emerge to bicycle off to an interesting meeting of the Fabian Society.

PERHAPS the imminence of the twentieth century that produced among thoughtful and artistic people a feeling that the new era, which was confidently hoped would be one of unexampled peace and progress and which the cultured and businesslike French were already preparing to usher in with yet another Exposition Universelle, should be provided with a suitable modern style of decoration. Such a style, it was generally considered, should clearly and unequivocally mark a break with the immediate past and therefore the plainer it was the greater would be the contrast. Fortunately the foundations of this style were ready to hand, laid by devoted Artists and Craftsmen in the byways of Chelsea and the valleys of the Cotswolds who had been living the simple life according to the doctrines of William Morris, surrounded by hand-woven linens, vegetable dyed, and plain unstained oak furniture by " goode workmen wel ywrought."

At first, while the control of the movement remained in English hands, something of the original simplicity was still maintained, albeit a remarkably self-conscious and uncomfortable simplicity ; but once the eager designers of Paris and Munich got their hands on it the result was nightmare. And as soon as the English decorators realized that at last this country had produced a style that had at once earned the approbation of the continent— where, just to make things easier, it was known as " le Modern style "— they too cast restraint to the winds. In less than no time a tangle of water-lilies cast their tenuous roots from ceiling to floor ; chairs, tables, mantelpieces, as though they had swallowed the White Rabbit's potion, shot skywards with a rapidity that rivalled Alice's ; in letters of a tortuous and illegible craftiness suitable mottoes, punctuated with tiny hearts, were beaten on copper and incised with pokers on wood ; and hand-made pots of an asymmetrical bulbousness that rendered them entirely useless for any practical purpose supported with difficulty a spray of honesty or a single iris. Here and there on the walls were displayed a few of the rare pictures which could possibly compete with the decoration ; Japanese prints the size of postage stamps in mounts like table-cloths, a Beardsley drawing or two and possibly a Whistler nocturne.

So extraordinary a style requires some explanation and it may not be too fanciful to assume the existence of a recurrent passion for tortuous curves and sinuous lines deeply embedded in the sub-conscious of the European artist, which from time to time finds expression in such exoticisms as the flamboyant Gothic of the later Middle Ages, mid-eighteenth-century Rococo and, most deplorable, in *Art Nouveau*. Certainly no style seems at first glance to provide a richer field for the investigations of Herr Freud.

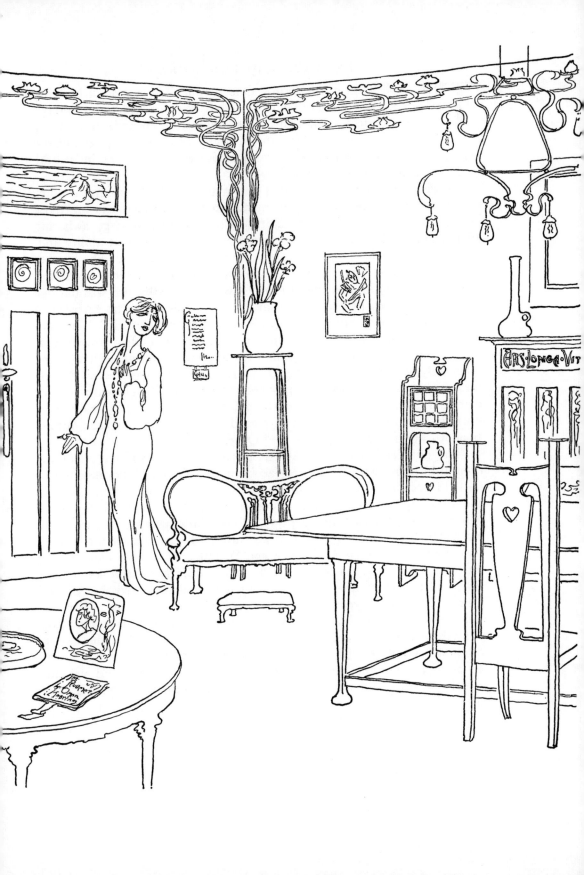

THE application of the term " Queen Anne " to a style of building which had not the most tenuous connection either with that sovereign or the architectural fashions of her reign would seem from a purely rational point of view to be as hard to justify as the employment of the Italian word for an open space to signify a covered balcony, and indeed the explanation is even more improbable.

As has been noted earlier, in the last quarter of the nineteenth century a certain *malaise* was discernible among English architects causing those affected perversely to abandon the true Gothic faith and to go awhoring after strange styles. Among them was a young man of great ability and, to some of his contemporaries, alarming versatility, Norman Shaw, who, more than anyone, was responsible for Pont Street Dutch which, as we have seen, contemporaries preferred to call Queen Anne. But this was but one of the styles which he promoted ; at the end of his career he emerged as the only begetter of Edwardian Baroque, and throughout his life he continued to produce numerous country houses, steeply gabled, heavily dormered, and occasionally turreted, in a vaguely Jacobean style which proved immensely popular both among architects and with the customers. Nevertheless, as it had been with his pastiches of the English eighteenth century that he had first caught the eye of the public, his whole output, and that of his numerous followers, continued, regardless of any petty stylistic distinctions, to be known henceforth as " Queen Anne."

The taste and scholarship which Norman Shaw invariably displayed even in his most extravagant neo-Jacobean fantasies had little influence on his followers and imitators (with the notable exception of Lutyens), but for the tile-hung gable-ends, the white-wood balconies and all the other trimmings they " went " in a big way. Soon almost every resort, and many residential areas, could boast a wide variety of examples of this strange style, half-way between *Art Nouveau* and Wimbledon Transitional. It was, for some inscrutable reason, judged to be particularly suitable for the seaside, and it was essentially as a holiday style that it crossed the Atlantic. Once arrived it enjoyed immediate and widespread popularity. Not only did it provide the local carpenter with a whole set of new and, on the whole, less exhausting opportunities for displaying his virtuosity, than those set by Hudson River Bracketed, but with no other style of building was it so easy to accommodate the innumerable and extensive porches and verandas which the American way of life had come increasingly to demand.

EDWARDIAN BAROQUE

AS soon as the Boer War had been brought to satisfactory conclusion and the seventh Edward was safely seated on his throne, the country entered upon a brief but glittering Indian summer of prosperity and glory; and in order adequately to express the Imperial grandeurs of this epoch it was generally felt that some new and grandiose style of architecture was called for. It was soon decided that the style most suitable for the task of turning the capital of the British Empire into a bigger and better Potsdam was a modified form of Baroque.

Soon many of the principal streets of London were rendered ominous by the erection of numerous buildings of terrifying proportions and elephantine decoration. Beneath circular windows the size of the Round Pond (copied from Hampton Court, for it was thought proper to introduce a patriotic note here and there) vast swags of brobdingnagian fruit sprawled across the façade, threatening all beneath with instant annihilation should their security have been overestimated by the architect. In attitudes of acute discomfort, nymphs and tribal deities of excessive female physique and alarming size balanced precariously on broken pediments, threatening the passer-by with a shower of stone fruit from the cavernous interiors of their inevitable cornucopia.

Alongside this neo-Baroque style in architecture there developed a characteristic form of Edwardian Rococo in interior decoration which was not only decidedly less offensive but occasionally even achieved a certain tinselly but appropriate, if specious, charm, of which few examples have, alas, survived. Only the other day the exquisite plaster-work in the main hall at Harrods was wantonly destroyed to make way for some tasteful modernistic improvements, but a few traces of decoration dating from this period are still visible in the baby-linen department. To-day almost the sole remaining masterpiece of the style is the restaurant and entrance-hall of the Ritz Hotel.

APART from *Art Nouveau*, of which the vogue was mercifully but not unnaturally limited, the main decorative influence in Edwardian period was French. And just as the dining-room was the key apartment of the Victorian era, and the studio of the immediately post-war decade, so the boudoir, significantly enough, was the characteristic region of the house in this silver age of European culture. This French influence took the familiar mid-eighteenth-century form, but with a wholeheartedness that produced what almost amounted to a full-dress Rococo revival. Walls were once more divided into damask-filled panels ; ceilings and cornices came out in a rash of plasterwork ; gilt easels groaned beneath the burden of untrustworthy Greuzes and dubious Bouchers ; and the floor was always covered with what was piously hoped to be an Aubusson. A legion of little ornaments still required a quantity of occasional tables for their accommodation but now tended to fall into two categories—the admittedly precious and the supposedly functional. In the former were included all the usual knick-knacks, with the addition of as many specimens of the ingenious Mons. Fabergé's costly handiwork as the owner could afford, while the latter embraced a large variety of musical instruments, which might or might not be played, and such happy symbols of the alliance of art and industry as lamp-supporting bronze nudes and voluptuous nereids twined round ink-pots. At the same time the stream of silver-framed photographs attained the dimensions of a flood engulfing every piece of furniture in the room. A particularly happy idea for the display of these tokens of family affection or social grandeur was to scatter them wholesale among the palms and other potted plants of a suitable robustness, which still retained all their old popularity. Thus one could frequently espy many a tiara'd dowager or bemedalled hussar peeping, jaguar like, from beneath the tropical undergrowth, while in all the best houses from the most prominent branch a pouchy and familiar eye, separated by a well-kept beard from a glossy expanse of waistcoat across which a condescending hand had scrawled " Edward R.," surveyed the world with a glance of slightly baleful *bonhomie*.

EDWARDIAN

TO-DAY the epithet Edwardian has perhaps acquired, thanks to Miss Sackville-West's charmingly expressed nostalgia, and the prodigious memoir-writing feats of the surviving Edwardians, a rather too exclusively aristocratic application. Its syllables summon up for most of us a confused vision of electric broughams, the portraits of Laszlo and Sargent, Patti in *Manon*, Homburg and Miss Cornwallis West. In fact this glorious vision, in so far as it corresponds in any degree with reality, is illumined by the after-glow of the Victorian era while the cheerful rays of the new dawn (subsequently discovered to be false) with which the majority of Edwardians considered the reign to have been ushered in, fall on a totally different collection of symbols.

Large areas of shiny white paint, masking the mahogany dear to the previous generation ; sticky-looking but cheerful chintzes patterned with large cabbage roses on a white background ; the beautiful and moving pictures of Herr Böcklin, made available to a large public through the commercial acumen of the Berlin Photographic Company ; these, together with the early plays of Mr. Shaw and the novels of Mr. Meredith, were some of the more characteristic signs of the times. But in addition there was one trait, which found ample expression in the contemporary interior, that particularly distinguishes the Edwardians from their immediate forebears— their pathetic faith in the benefits of science.

Soon the home was invaded by an entirely new collection of furniture and fittings in the design of most of which the supporters of *Art Nouveau*, by no means yet moribund, had secured an unfortunate monopoly. From the heart of a tinted glass flower at the end of a terrifyingly sinuous brass stalk there now peeped the electric light-bulb, while in the fireplace a strange collection of stalactites, in a black lead sarcophagus embossed with a design of water lilies, glowed with gas-produced heat. Pendent from the wall a complicated contraption of vulcanite, mahogany and polished brass carried the householder's voice, at the mere turning of a handle, to such of his neighbours as were similarly equipped, while the hanging book-case, itself a striking testimony to little Willy's skill with that popular scientific toy the fret-saw, groaned beneath its load of Mr. Wells's marvellous romances. Everything in the garden, to use a contemporary phrase, was lovely.

And then one day the largest and most impressive miracle of modern science hit an iceberg in mid-Atlantic, and the prevailing optimism received a shock which two years later was repeated on a scale and at a length sufficient to banish it for ever.

THE post-war era, from the social historian's point of view, started some time previous to that fatal afternoon at Serajevo. The truth of this tiresomely paradoxical statement is borne out by the number of phenomena that we have come to regard as particularly characteristic of the roaring 'twenties which were, in fact, flourishing in the first two years of His late Majesty's reign. Female emancipation, jazz, bright young people, large-scale labour disputes, cubism, the gowns of Mons. Poiret, Diaghilev's Russian Ballet, all made their first appearance in a world in which any existing war-weariness dated from the Boer War.

Of all these startling and varied developments by far the most important in the realm of interior decoration was undoubtedly the last. So far-reaching were the changes that this remarkable theatrical venture brought about in the drawing-rooms of the great world that Napoleon's conquest of Egypt (which also littered the *salons* of London and Paris with boat-loads of exotic bric-à-brac) provides the only possible, although inadequate, parallel. Before one could say Nijinsky the pale pastel shades which had reigned supreme on the walls of Mayfair for almost two decades were replaced by a riot of barbaric hues—jade green, purple, every variety of crimson and scarlet, and, above all, orange. Gone were the Hubert Roberts and the Conder fans and their place was taken by the costume designs of Bakst and the theatre scenes of Benois. The Orient came once more into its own and the piano was draped with Chinese shawls, the divan replaced the chaise-longue and no mantelpiece was complete without its Buddha.

Not the least of the Russian Ballets achievements was the social kudos it acquired for art. Throughout the nineteenth century the aristocracy had displayed an ever-increasing dislike of culture (such æsthetic movements as those of the 'seventies and 'eighties flourished far more abundantly in the neighbourhood of the Cromwell Road than round about Park Lane), but now Art came once more to roost among the duchesses, where it was at length productive of a wave of modified Bohemianism. This produced a tendency to regard a room not so much as a place to live in, but as a setting for a party, with the result that the studio (so easy to run in a time of acute servant shortage) was suddenly much in demand for purely residential purposes.

Significantly enough, that happy acceptance of the wonders of science, which had been such a feature of the Edwardian age, vanished along with the flowered chintzes and the overmantel, and the electric light now took refuge in an old Chinese temple lantern and the telephone lurked coyly beneath the capacious skirts of a Russian peasant doll, dressed after a design by Goncharova.

WHILE the drawing-rooms of the upper and middle classes underwent a variety of changes in the years between the Great Exhibition and the General Strike, the decoration of the average cottage remained very much the same, and even now, in the age of cheap furniture on the instalment plan and functional flats for the proletariat, there still exist in remote districts a few specimens, as yet untenanted by intellectuals, in which the old style is still worthily displayed.

Against a waxed wall-paper, dark in hue and boldly floral in design, are ranged innumerable ornaments and pictures, for the true cottager still retains that passion for objects, which the cultured have so signally abandoned. Oleographs of deceased sovereigns and the late Lord Roberts, comic cats with the arms of Weston-super-Mare lavishly emblazoned on their buttocks, photographic mementoes of long-forgotten bean-feasts jostle one another on the bobble-fringed mantelpiece, while among the numerous trophies of rod and gun, artistically mounted, and hand-tinted camera studies of the dear deceased, the flower entwined Gothic lettering of some pithy saying from the scriptures strikes a welcome note of lettered piety. And on the round central table and the window-sill a striking collection of potted ferns testifies to a natural interest in horticulture.

K

IN earlier and less enlightened times the majority of cottages were inhabited by landworkers and a sprinkling of retired retainers spending the evening of their days in the modest rural comfort provided by the large-hearted nobility and gentry whom they had served. In the period between the wars this simple pattern was increasingly modified. Nine out of ten country cottages (that is, the more sanitary and comfortable nine) came to be occupied by writers, film stars, barristers, artists and B.B.C. announcers, and as a result the interior decoration of the average cottage underwent considerable modification.

The flowered wall-paper, shiny with wax, was replaced by hygienic distemper of an artistic pastel shade ; the plastic souvenirs of famous seaside resorts banished in favour of genuine examples of peasant handicrafts coming from Czecho-Slovakia by way of an interesting little shop, run by gentlefolk, in the Brompton Road. The oleographs and tinted camera studies disappeared and their place was taken by hand-printed rhyme sheets, clever little woodcuts and expansive reproductions of those ubiquitous sunflowers. No longer was the Family Bible visible on a richly covered centre table ; instead " A Shropshire Lad " (hand-printed edition on rag paper, signed by the author and limited to two hundred copies), occupied an " accidentally " conspicuous position on an " artist designed " table of unstained oak.

However, so extraordinary are the workings of taste and fashion that in recent years there has been a return among the ultra-sophisticated to the genuine cottage interior ; but needless to say the aspidistra is worn with a difference. Photographs of late-Victorian wedding-groups return to the walls, but they owe their position not to any sudden excess of family feeling but to their allegedly humorous qualities. Similarly steel-engravings and wax fruit enjoy a come-back on an " amusing " basis. At first sight an extremely simple observer might imagine that the Victorians were back, but it would not be long before he realized that all these symbols are firmly displayed between inverted commas.

During the course of the first European war the eighteenth century, as a source of inspiration, was almost completely neglected. This was not altogether unnatural, for that golden age, still surrounded as it was by a happy haze of Edwardian wishful thinking which conveniently blurred its less attractive aspects, now appeared singularly remote from the unpleasant realities of war-time Europe. (People were apt to forget that the age of Crébillon and Fragonard was also the age of Frederick the Great and Maréchal Saxe.) Moreover, we were all still fighting to make the world safe for democracy—an ideal which would have exercised almost no appeal for the contemporaries of the Earl of Chatham. It was not surprising therefore that, in so far as the decorative arts continued to flourish, the exotic charms and barbaric colour schemes popularized by our gallant Russian allies reigned supreme.

Once the war was over, however, and it became obvious that the democracy for which we had striven was neither so safe nor so agreeable as many people had optimistically assumed, the aristocratic qualities, which eighteenth-century culture had so successfully embodied, soon regained their old appeal. But this new revival, owing largely to the writings of the talented brothers Sitwell, differed considerably from that which had flourished in Edwardian times. Now it was Italy, and to a lesser extent Spain and southern Germany, which provided the model. Gone were the Louis Seize chairs and the Largillière portraits, and their place was taken by innumerable pieces of hand-painted furniture from Venice and a surprisingly abundant supply of both the Canalettos. At the same time a markedly ecclesiastical note is struck by the forests of twisted baroque candlesticks, willingly surrendered by countless Italian padres (in exchange for the wherewithal with which to purchase up-to-date machine-turned brass electroliers), old leather-bound hymn-books cunningly hollowed out to receive cigarettes, and exuberant gilt *prie-dieu* ingeniously transformed into receptacles for gramophone records. And all the little Fabergé knick-knacks and Dresden china shepherdesses are finally routed by a noble army of martyrs from the Salzkammergut whose plaster writhings are rendered properly decorative by a liberal application of iridescent paint.

THE most remarkable development in urban domestic architecture during the inter-war period was undoubtedly the rapid popularization of the large block of flats. Hitherto the English, almost alone among European nations, had resolutely refused to become flat-minded, but during the 'twenties and 'thirties of the present century the acute shortage of domestic servants, the sedulous aping among all classes of everything American, the appalling rise in the rates and an increased familiarity with the works of Dr. Marie Stopes led to a wholesale abandonment of the capacious and dignified mansions which had been the pride of the upper and middle classes in Victorian times in favour of these labour-saving cliff dwellings which between the wars sprang up in all the residential districts of the capital to the total ruination of the skyline.

The modern flat falls into one or other of two categories; either it is "self-contained" or it is "luxury." The first class (so called because it contains the owner's self and nothing else), is usually divided into a bed-sitting-room, a kitchenette (a word which reveals with sad clarity the state of modern culture) and a bathroom. It usually fulfils its claim of saving labour by being so abominably ill-planned that no respectable domestic can be induced to work in it. The luxury flat, on the other hand, with little or no more floor space than the self-contained variety, is divided up with fiendish ingenuity into a dining-room, drawing-room, lounge-hall, three bed, two bath, a kitchen and all the usual offices.

Apart from their planning both varieties have much in common. In each case the bathroom is by far the largest room in the flat, the walls are so thin that a radio on the ground floor is clearly audible at the top of the block, and such rooms as do not look out on to an interior well faced with glazed lavatory bricks invariably face the largest and busiest traffic thoroughfare in the immediate neighbourhood.

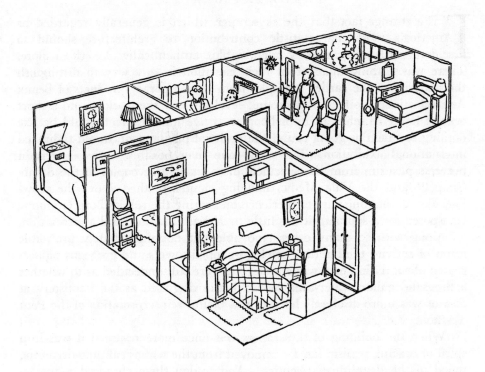

IT is a strange fact that the skyscraper which is generally regarded as America's most characteristic contribution to architecture should so seldom strike any readily identifiable, authentically American note. There was nothing apart from their elevation in any way to distinguish the majority of the earlier examples from contemporary products of Beaux Arts eclecticism going up at ground level all over the world ; and a short tour of lower Manhattan by helicopter at five hundred feet would be like nothing so much as going round the national pavilions at an old-fashioned international exhibition. But while one may possibly derive a certain perverse pleasure from the spectacle of so many free copies of the Sainte Chapelle and the Villa Medici hanging cloud-wreathed above the snow-line, akin to that one might experience on hearing the rôle of Boris Godunov transposed for a soprano, it has little to do with architectural appreciation.

Along with so many other enjoyable but not immediately profitable forms of activity the building of cloud-capped towers and gorgeous palaces ceased abruptly in 1929, while architects were still undecided as to whether a thousand gallon water-tank looked better disguised as the baptistery at Pisa or was more discreetly housed in a tactful reinterpretation of the Petit Trianon.

When the building of skyscrapers was once more resumed it was in a spirit of bracing realism far, far removed from the whimsical pipe-dreaming mood of the dear, dead twenties. And to-day these clustered pinnacles from which so many keen followers of the Stock Market took their final plunge, admittedly immensely effective as landscape (when seen from the sea, for instance), if not as architecture, are as much period pieces as the speak-easy and the ukelele.

DESPITE the international fame achieved by *Art Nouveau* its appeal had nevertheless been limited to a comparatively small coterie of Simple Lifers, Homespinners, Fabians, Suffragettes and the fifty-seven other fascinating varieties of British Intellectual. But as the new century advanced many of its features were introduced, not indeed in their original purity, to a far wider public. To meet the demands created by the rapid suburban development of London, more particularly in the south-western districts, a style was evolved which for lack of a better name we shall refer to as Wimbledon Transitional, which in its plentiful use of pebble-dash, its giddy treatment of gables and its general air of self conscious cosiness is plainly revealed as the unattractive offspring of *Art Nouveau*. Moreover, various other features of the style—for example, the fiendish variety of surface materials (frequently one finds pebbledash, ridge-tiling, fancy brickwork, weather-boarding and half-timbering all employed on the outside walls of the same building)—suggest that the other partner in the disgraceful liaison that gave it birth was none other than our old friend Pont Street Dutch.

However, it would be wrong to suppose that Wimbledon Transitional was a purely derivative style, for two of its most striking features had at the time an air of striking novelty. First, the skilful but unrestrained use of white painted wooden balconies, porches and verandas ; second, the revival of half-timbering, a method of building which had been allowed to remain in a state of well-merited neglect for nearly three centuries. Thus Wimbledon Transitional occupies a position of peculiar importance in the history of modern British architecture, as being the connecting link between Pont Street Dutch and *Art Nouveau*, and such familiar modern styles as Stock-brokers' Tudor and By-pass Variegated.

It is important to remember that at the time of its inception Wimbledon Transitional was essentially an upper-class style and attained its finest development in the £1,500–£2,000 a year districts of Surrey and the South Coast. It is still possible to find many splendid examples in these neigh-bourhoods that retain their original setting of conifers and rhododendrons and to see them at their best the serious student is advised to time his visit for sundown, when the pebbledash and the brickwork are bathed in a rich rosy glow and the Wellingtonias stand out black and menacing against the evening sky.

ONE of the less happy, but unfortunately more widespread, results of the Arts and Crafts, Simple Life, Back to Nature movements which flourished so exceedingly in the period between the Jubilee and the first European War was a passionate longing for rusticity. The Englishman's home need no longer be his castle but it must at all costs (even when it is within easy reach of the City) be his country cottage. Thus urban domestic architecture soon ceased to exist and in all the outer districts of London its place was taken by row upon row of rural retreats bearing no conceivable relation either to each other or the streets into which they were crowded.

In the most striking and expensive of the early varieties of this semi-rustic revival, which for convenience we have classified as Wimbledon Transitional, the country-house atmosphere is even more overwhelming within than without. Here the lounge-hall reaches the ultimate peak of its development. From an impressive landing, always referred to as the gallery, a flight of polished oak stairs lead down to a gleaming parquet sea on which float a variety of rich Turkey rugs. Light and air, the former in small quantities, the latter in unlimited supplies, are admitted through a bewildering selection of doors and French windows which one constantly expects (such is the theatrical complexity of their arrangement) to fly open and reveal the pyjama-clad forms of Mr. Robertson Hare or Mr. Ralph Lynn. On the walls, or rather such part of them as is not covered by a wealth of old oak panelling, hang long lines of sporting prints, punctuated here and there by a barometer or a warming-pan, testifying to the strong sporting instincts of the squirearchy of Metroland.

Although in real life the popularity of this style of decoration has waned considerably of recent years, its predominance remains unchallenged in certain sections of the theatre owing to the fact that it provides an equally convenient setting for the gay philanderer on his amorous prowl from bedroom to bedroom and for the third most dangerous man in Europe desperately trying to conceal the corpse of the Chinese butler before the end of Act II.

Needless to say this style, which first appeared in the early 1900's, is still regarded as the last word in up-to-date elegance in film circles where it provides the invariable background for all scenes of English high-life.

JUDGED by medieval standards of comfort the domestic buildings of the sixteenth century were doubtless almost luxurious; by any other criterion they had little to recommend them. The exigencies of timber construction kept the rooms low and cramped; the expense of glazing ensured that the windows would be few and small; and their claim to be considered beautiful can only be allowed on the grounds of sentiment or an undying attachment to the picturesque. Nevertheless, so deep and so widespread was the post-war devotion to the olde-worlde that an enormous number of such houses were erected, at considerable expense (for the methods of building general in Tudor times are nowadays as uneconomic as they are unnecessary), and the greatest ingenuity was displayed in providing the various modern devices with which they were anachronistically equipped with suitable olde-worlde disguises. Thus electrically produced heat warmed the hands of those who clustered enthusiastically round the yule-logs blazing so prettily in the vast hearth; the light which shone so cosily from the old horn lantern was obtained from the grid; and from the depths of some old iron-bound chest were audible the dulcet tones of Mr. Bing Crosby or the old-world strains of Mr. Duke Ellington.

But worse was to come. At first, as noticed above, the expense had been considerable and prevented the adoption of the style by all but high-class builders working for wealthy clients, but soon the invention of new and cheaper methods of production brought it within the reach of the builders of Metroland. And to-day when the young passer-by is a little unnerved at being suddenly confronted with a hundred and fifty accurate reproductions of Anne Hathaway's cottage, each complete with central-heating and garage, he should pause to reflect on the extraordinary fact that all over the country the latest and most scientific methods of mass-production were, only a few years ago, still being utilized to turn out a stream of old oak beams, leaded window-panes and small discs of bottle-glass, all structural devices which our ancestors lost no time in abandoning as soon as an increase in wealth and knowledge enabled them to do so.

"Four posts round my bed,
Oake beames overhead,
Olde rugges on ye floor,
No stockbroker could aske for more."

Sussex house-agent's song.
(*Traditional, early twentieth century.*)

IN interior decoration the antiquarian enthusiast's cherished ideal, relentlessly and all too successfully pursued, was a glorified version of Anne Hathaway's cottage, with such mass-produced modifications as were necessary to conform to transatlantic standards of plumbing. In construction the Tudor note was truly sounded : in the furnishing considerable deviations from strict period accuracy were permissible. Thus eighteenth-century four-posters, Regency samplers, and Victorian chintzes all soon came to be regarded as Tudor by adoption—at least in estate agency circles.

Soon certain classes of the community were in a position to pass their whole lives in one long Elizabethan daydream ; spending their nights under high-pitched roofs and ancient eaves, their days in trekking from Tudor golf clubs to half-timbered cocktail bars, and their evenings in contemplating Mr. Laughton's robust interpretation of Henry VIII amid the Jacobean plasterwork of the Gloriana Palace.

It was foolishly supposed at the time that the height of absurdity had finally been reached shortly before the Second World War when it was seriously proposed to build an exact reproduction—only naturally three times the size—of the original Globe Theatre in Southwark to which patrons were to be ferried across the river in Elizabethan skiffs rowed by Elizabethan seamen.

However, this fortunately never-achieved triumph of misplaced ingenuity paled beside the actuality of the half-timbered buffet cars with which soon after the war British Railways equipped certain of their more widely publicized express trains.

L

IN the troubled times in which we live it is perhaps not unnatural that many a longing glance should be cast at those periods of the past of which we like to persuade ourselves a profound tranquillity was the keynote. Nor is it surprising that no class of the community should have been so deeply affected by this form of nostalgia as the bankers, although it must be admitted that the period of their choice, the eighteenth century, bore in actual fact little or no resemblance to the roast-beef and Reynolds, gilt-edged and candle-lit world of their dreams. However, solidity was the quality they sought and solidity was the quality with which they retrospectively endowed the age of the French Revolution. It was not the first time that wish-fulfilment has operated in the formation of an architectural style.

The architects who were favoured had, as a rule, rather less understanding of the nature and practice of eighteenth-century architecture than the bankers who employed them, and the resulting style, known as Bankers' Georgian, always preserves something of the air of a Metro-Goldwyn-Mayer production of the *School for Scandal* ; a certain restlessness arising from the knowledge that no expense is to be spared, but at the same time refinement must remain the watchword. Moreover, owing possibly to the fact that one of the masters of the style hailed from the outposts of Empire, a curious provincialism is frequently discernible, particularly in the treatment of detail which, while it brings a bracing whiff of the veldt into the stuffy atmosphere of Lombard Street, does little to preserve the illusion of the eighteenth century.

Even after the war Bankers' Georgian remained popular, and hundreds of examples are still visible in London and the provinces. Apart from a suspicious newness and a superabundance of plate-glass the almost invariable feature by which it can easily be distinguished from the genuine article is the high-pitched bogus-Mansard roof. It should not, however, be confused with the two related but yet distinct styles, Office of Works Queen Anne and Architectural Association (or Beggars' Opera) Georgian. The latter may readily be distinguished by its invincible refinement while the former always preserves an unmistakable air of having just been run-up by the little woman round the corner.

WATERTIGHT GUARANTY TRUST Co. Inc.

THIS style, which attained great popularity between the wars, is actually our old friend Pont Street Dutch with a few Stockholm trimmings and a more daring use of colour. In the most typical examples the walls are whitewashed, the roof is covered with Roman tiles in a peculiarly vehement shade of green, and the windows have been enriched with a great deal of fancy leading of a tortuous ingenuity. It was the upper-class style *par excellence* of the pre-slump years, but latterly has sunk a little in the social scale and occasional examples are now to be found alongside some of our more exclusive by-passes.

Within, the decoration was almost always carried out in Curzon Street ecclesiastical-Spanish with a plentiful supply of Knole sofas, large baroque candlesticks fitted with lampshades made out of old sheets of music or maps, and an occasional wrought-iron grille. The walls were usually stippled in peach or sea-green hues and sometimes ingenious tricks of shading were employed. It provided the invariable background against which the characters in Messrs. Lonsdale's and Coward's earlier plays cracked their epigrams and its presence may always be assumed in the novels of Mr. Arlen.

While it was essentially a country-house style and many of its greatest masterpieces are located on the sea-coast, a few examples are to be found in the more expensive suburbs of the capital and it can be studied in all its diversity in the neighbourhood of Hampstead.

IN the years immediately after the first German War there raged on both sides of the Atlantic a strange enthusiasm for all things Spanish, which resulted, on one level, in the increased appreciation of the paintings of Greco and the music of de Falla and, on another, in a rush of tortoiseshell combs to the head and the staggering popularity of the late Rudolf Valentino in *The Four Horsemen of the Apocalypse*. In England it was confined, in its architectural manifestation, to the adoption of Curzon Street Baroque for interior decoration and a scattering of wrought-iron grilles over unsuitable facades. But in America, where the boom years saw what was almost certainly the last great period in which the theory of conspicuous consumption reigned unchallenged in the field of domestic building, and where a handful of dilapidated Spanish missions provided an unconvincing historical justification, Hispanophilism carried all before it.

Through heraldry-laden porticoes friends of the Great Gatsby swept in their Cadillacs into colonnaded patios ablaze with azulejo tiles ; from baroque belfries convent bells summoned the guests to synthetic gin mixed in genuine holy-water stoups ; down flights of balustraded stairs copied, or in some cases removed bodily, from the palaces of Seville and Salamanca Flaming Youth tottered to its doom.

While it was undoubtedly in Florida, where that great cultural force, the late Addison Mizener, was then enjoying his hey-day as architect and real-estate operator, and where the sought-for illusion gained a certain measure of support from the climate and vegetation, that the style was most richly developed, examples are numerous throughout the States. Custom-built haciendas sprang up almost overnight throughout the length of the West Coast clustering particularly thickly in those residential areas favoured by the big names of the film world, and even the austere beauty of the New England landscape was occasionally enriched by a touch of Southern grace. For above the chilly waters of Long Island Sound the skyline is surprisingly broken by the clustering turrets and open belfries of the Hohenschwangau of the Vanderbilts, where enshrined saints and chirurgeresque detail, applied, apparently, in some form of solidified tooth-paste squeezed from a tube, proclaim an unshaken devotion to Hispanic ideals far from favouring palms and concealing bougainvilia—the last great manifestation (parts of it date from as late as 1936), and it must be admitted an unworthy one, of that romantic passion for architectural make-believe which had started with the Brighton Pavilion.

IF an architect of enormous energy, painstaking ingenuity and great structural knowledge, had devoted years of his life to the study of the problem of how best to achieve the maximum of inconvenience, in the shape and arrangement under one roof of a stated number of rooms, and had had the assistance of a corps of research workers ransacking architectural history for the least attractive materials and building devices known in the past, it is just possible, although highly unlikely, that he might have evolved a style as crazy as that with which the speculative builder, at no expenditure of mental energy at all, has enriched the landscape on either side of our great arterial roads. As one passes by one can amuse one's self by classifying the various contributions which past styles have made to this infernal amalgam ; here are some quaint gables culled from *Art Nouveau* surmounting a façade that is plainly Modernistic in inspiration ; there the twisted beams and leaded panes of Stockbrokers' Tudor are happily contrasted with bright green tiles of obviously Pseudish origin ; next door some terra-cotta plaques, Pont Street Dutch in character, enliven a white wood Wimbledon Transitional porch, making it a splendid foil to a red-brick garage that is vaguely Romanesque in feeling. But while he is heavily indebted to history for the majority of his decorative and structural details (in almost every case the worst features of the style from which they were filched), in the planning and disposition of his erections the speculative builder displays a genius that is all his own. Notice the skill with which the houses are disposed, that insures that the largest possible area of country-side is ruined with the minimum of expense ; see how carefully each householder is provided with a clear view into the most private offices of his next-door neighbour and with what studied disregard of the sun's aspect the principal rooms are planned.

It is sad to reflect that so much ingenuity should have been wasted on streets and estates which will inevitably become the slums of the future. That is, if a fearful and more sudden fate does not obliterate them prematurely.

NO architectural development of our time has done so much to change the face of our cities and indirectly to alter the whole tempo of our social life as the coming of the large block of luxury flats. As a means of housing a large number of people in a crowded urban area it has much to recommend it, but unfortunately, owing to a variety of causes, it has been accorded a hearty welcome at the wrong end of the social scale. As a result, those residential districts such as Mayfair, which are of the greatest interest architecturally, have been ruthlessly cut up in order to make way for truncated red-brick tenement buildings, which may quite possibly with the addition of another thirty stories achieve a certain monumental impressiveness in the neighbourhood of Park Avenue, but which are completely unsuited to Park Lane ; while the inhabitants of other districts which should long ago have been demolished are forced, if they wish to move, to trek out to the scabrous housing estates that are rapidly devouring what remains of the open spaces in the home counties.

The most extraordinary feature of the whole business, however, remains the fantastic illogicality which prompts those who could well afford comfortable and dignified homes to live in a collection of centrally-heated matchboxes in a building resembling a pickle-factory inconsequently decorated with a few stage props left over from a provincial production of *The Beggars' Opera*, carefully situated at the noisiest corner of the busiest available thoroughfare, and at a rental three times the cost of running all but the most grandiose town house.

THE increasingly numerous blocks of working-class flats, although similar in many respects to the Park Lane variety, are nevertheless easily distinguishable by reason of a number of interesting features. First, they are always situated in a much quieter neighbourhood ; secondly, the rents are much lower though the rooms are seldom any smaller ; thirdly, they are usually rather better architecturally. True, they too look like pickle-factories, but quite good pickle-factories ; not, it must be admitted, owing to any particular skill on the part of the architect, but solely to the fact that there has not been sufficient money to waste on Portland stone facings and other decorative trimmings. The convenience of the tenants is a consideration that is invariably treated with the same lordly disregard in both varieties.

If, however, you are still in doubt as to which category any particular block of flats belongs (for occasionally it so happens that the builders of Park Lane blocks are at a loss to find a really noisy site and local authorities are sometimes in a position to push up the rates and so afford a few decorative urns and a lot of fancy tiling) it is advisable to see what name is inscribed over the entrance ; in nine cases out of ten, if it has " buildings " tacked on it is a working-class block, whereas if it has " house " it comes under the luxury heading. If all else fails, see if there are any trees in the immediate neighbourhood ; if there are, it may undoubtedly be classified as L.C.C., as there is nothing which the luxury flat architect hates so much as a tree, and not only will he take great care not to plant any but will go to infinite trouble to ensure the destruction of any that may already be there.

WHEN, shortly after the First World War, the Modern Movement (q.v.) was first brought to the public notice it led to a natural and healthy reaction against the excessive ornament with which the architects of the previous generation had so abundantly enriched their façades ; but unfortunately a great number of architects and builders, being completely out of sympathy with the ideals of the true supporters of the movements, wasted no time in happily turning this novel simplicity to their own ends. The great advantage, in their eyes, of these large expanses of plain wall free from the burden of heavy cornices, swags of fruit and elaborate rustication, lay in the splendid surface they presented for the application of a whole new series of ornaments, more cheery in appearance and more expressive of the tastes of the age of jazz. Thus the buildings which cultured and disinterested men had at length succeeded in freeing from the burden of out-worn academic impedimenta were now enlivened by the addition of quite meaningless scrolls and whirls in a fiendish variety of materials, ranging from chromium plate to bakelite, which the ingenuity of modern science had placed at the disposal of every tuppenny-hapenny builder in the country. So the last state of British architecture was even worse than the first, for the earlier forms of applied decoration, hideous, misused and unnecessary as they had become, had at least some thin, tenuous connection with a once vital tradition, whereas these bars of beaten copper, these sheets of black glass, these friezes of chromium pomegranates, not only did not arise out of the demands of construction but had not the slightest shred of tradition to provide a threadbare excuse for their revolting existence.

Numerous examples of the Modernistic are to be found in all our principal cities, and such of our great luxury cinemas as are not built in Metro-Goldwyn Renaissance are almost without exception conspicuous masterpieces of this style. Incidentally the Modernistic is not confined exclusively to architecture, but has made itself felt in the realm of interior decoration and has had a peculiarly disastrous effect on typography.

STAUNCHLY as the neo-Tudor enthusiasts waged their olde-worlde campaign, they were never able completely to stifle the opinions of those who held that the brave new world of the 'twenties and 'thirties demanded a brave new style. Desperate efforts were made to convince the architectural public that half-timbering and leaded panes were easily adaptable to the requirements of nine-storey blocks of flats, and that reinforced concrete methods of construction were ideally suited to support bigger and better beams ; but apart from one or two gargantuan luxury " Closes " the flat builders were disinclined to put these ideals into practice. They were therefore faced with the problem of evolving some style of interior decoration to harmonize with the bogus Hollywood modernism of the type of exterior which they preferred.

The resulting style was a nightmare amalgam of a variety of elements derived from several sources. The foundation was provided by that Jazz style which enjoyed a mercifully brief period of popularity in the immediate post-Versailles period, which was itself the fruit of a fearful union between the flashier side of Ballets Russes and a hopelessly vulgarized version of Cubism. To this were added elements derived from the *style colonial* popularized by the Paris Exhibition of 1927, such as an all too generous use of the obscure and more hideous woods, and a half-hearted simplicity that derived from a complete misunderstanding of the ideals of the Corbusier-Gropius school of architects and found uneasy expression in unvarnished wood and chromium plate, relentlessly misapplied.

It is significant that the old English fondness for disguising everything as something else now attained the dimensions of a serious pathological affliction. Gramophones masquerade as cocktail cabinets ; cocktail cabinets as book-cases ; radios lurk in tea-caddies and bronze nudes burst asunder at the waist-line to reveal cigarette lighters ; and nothing is what it seems. On reflection it is not perhaps surprising that disaster should have overtaken a generation which refused so consistently to look even the most ordinary facts in the face.

M

FROM the late eighteenth century onward social distinctions had always been clearly distinguishable in interior decoration. On the one hand there existed the vast mass of middle and upper middle-class homes in which the décor and furnishings seldom underwent any sudden drastic change but were slowly and almost imperceptibly modified from generation to generation. On the other there were a small number of ultra-smart householders who reacted instantaneously to every change of fashion and whose houses seldom presented the same appearance two years running. It was the latter class of patron who adopted and popularized such styles as first Russian Ballet and Curzon Street Baroque. A recent style to catch their fancy was Vogue Regency.

While there is little that one can say in favour of any attempt to re-create a vanished style in conditions totally different from those in which it first flourished, a revival of the decoration and furnishing tastes in favour in the first quarter of the last century has a rather more logical justification than most such antiquarian enthusiasms. The period between the Napoleonic wars and the upheavals of 1848 was like the inter-war period—one in which vast social and political changes took place and which witnessed the final disappearance of the old eighteenth-century culture that was already in decline. Moreover, the Regency style represents the last development of the classical tradition that started with Inigo Jones. It was followed and obliterated by a series of irrational and disastrous experiments, the outcome of the enthusiasms aroused by the Romantic Movement working through the media all too generously provided by the Industrial Revolution. To-day the more sensible of modern architects realize that the desperate attempt to find a contemporary style can only succeed if the search starts at the point where Soane left off.

Luckily the furniture of the Regency period possesses in an exceptional degree the quality of adaptability—it " goes " as well with a strapping pink nude by Picasso as with the less generously proportioned nymphs of David or Etty. And a Recamier sofa is in no way embarrassed by the close proximity of a rug by Marian Dorn. So long, therefore, as no attempt is made to follow the fatal will-o'-the-wisp of period accuracy, Vogue Regency remains as suitable a style as any for a period in describing which the word Transitional, it is now apparent, is the grossest of understatements.

"The history of civilization . . . leaves in architecture its truest, because its most unconscious, record."

HOWEVER, the late Mr. Geoffrey Scott when he wrote those words had not had the inestimable privilege of observing, in the late Herr Schickelgruber, the Architect as Man of Action. So that while the main contention expressed in the above sentence remains unassailable the subsidiary clause may be thought to stand in need of some slight modification. After all those speeches about building for the future, for generations of pure-bred Aryans yet unborn, can we still subscribe to the view that the record is always unconscious? Those gigantic pillars, those megalithic colonnades, that so obvious austerity, were they not designed with one eye on the future? With the fully conscious hope that posterity would say "Here was a race of supermen, the builders of a civilization that was moved by a stern and splendid purpose and buttressed by an unbelievable solidity"? Surely the architecture of the Third Reich was in the nature of a reinsurance clause that would compensate the noble Teuton for the crass stupidity that prevented his contemporaries from appreciating the nobility, firmness and idealism of his régime by making certain of the admiration of the future.

For, alas, the non-German had not been overwhelmed with admiration. He realized, unless blinded by ideology, that some of these buildings were not without merit—they frequently achieved a definite if rather empty dignity, with welcome freedom from fussy ornament—but he remembered that the whole thing had already been done a great deal better. Napoleon too had his creative whims and as an architectural expression of *sacro egoismo* the first Empire style, as developed in the layout and planning of Paris, makes the masterpieces of our latter-day dictators look empty, bombastic and ridiculous. It was, indeed, unfortunate for Herr Hitler that the German pavilion at the Paris Exhibition of 1936 should have been within a hundred miles of the Arc de Triomphe.

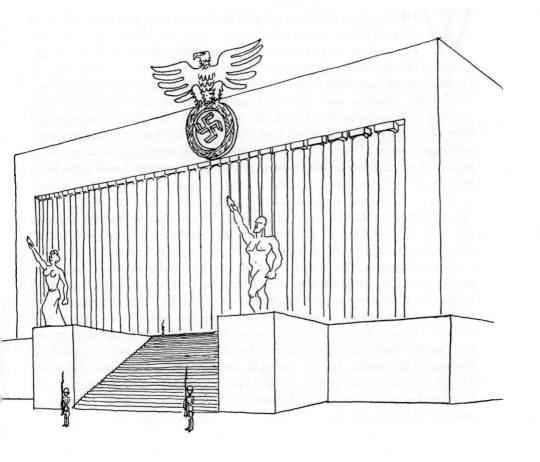

WHEN a New Age dawned and the Soviet state was born, we were all told by its many admirers that now we should see what the proletarian architect could accomplish when freed from the shackles of capitalistic patronage. This new freedom, it could not be doubted, would accomplish that for which architectural reformers had been striving for years, a new and vital architecture cleanly expressive of its purpose and unencumbered with all those fripperies which the degraded taste of an outworn civilization had clung to as symbols of bourgeois taste and importance. It was therefore all the more distressing, that after a long period of waiting the architecture which finally emerged should have been so difficult to distinguish from that produced by the less inspired academic architects working as wage-slaves of capitalism. But sad as was this disappointment, it was still more depressing when it was discovered that the minor details wherein it differed from the architecture of effete social-democracy were just those which strike an unbiased observer as being most reminiscent of the architecture of international Fascism. The same emphasis on size, the same tendency to imagine that beauty is to be achieved by merely abolishing ornament, regardless of the fact that it is dependent on the proportions of what is then revealed, the same declamatory and didactic idiom. There existed, of course, one or two very minor differences, such as the Soviet architect's habit of eschewing the use of the capital on ideological grounds ; but in essentials the two styles remained the same. The proletarian of this period and the Fascist both laboured under the same misapprehension—that political rhetoric is a sufficient substitute for genuine architectural inspiration.

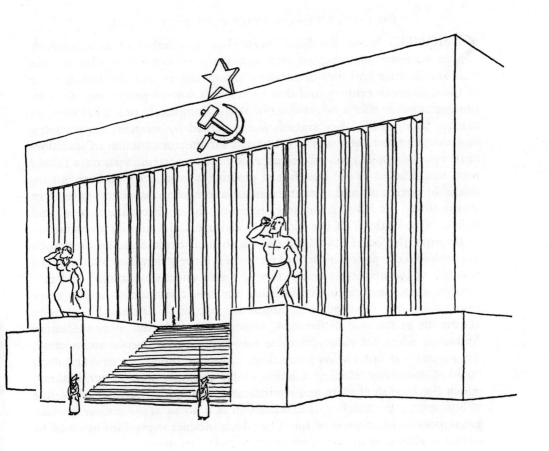

SHORTLY before the First World War a number of accomplished, disinterested and original architects came to the sad conclusion that architecture had died somewhere about the end of the first quarter of the nineteenth century and that therefore it was no longer any use continuing hopeless efforts at revival but that a completely new start must be made. Modern life, they argued, was governed by mechanical principles, and therefore the rules which held good for the construction of machines must now be applied to architecture. That this doctrine rests on a fallacy need not blind us to the fact that in practice it produced buildings of considerable merit and had a most excellent and revivifying effect on modern architecture. It led to a ruthless abandonment of all ornamentation, and although the example of the eighteenth century and antiquity are sufficient to disprove the belief that decoration is in itself deplorable, no ornaments are undoubtedly preferable to bad ones. Thus the style which now emerged was one of the utmost austerity, relying for its effect on planning and proportion alone, and faithfully fulfilling the one condition to which every importance was attached, of " fitness for purpose." Admirable as were the results in the case of factories, airports, hospitals and other utilitarian buildings, when the same principle was applied to domestic architecture, the success was not always so marked. For one thing, the new architects could seldom resist making a house fit for purposes such as sun-bathing, which the English climate and environment frequently rendered impossible of fulfilment ; for another, the conception of a house as *une machine à habiter* presupposes a barrenness of spirit to which, despite every indication of its ultimate achievement, we have not yet quite attained.

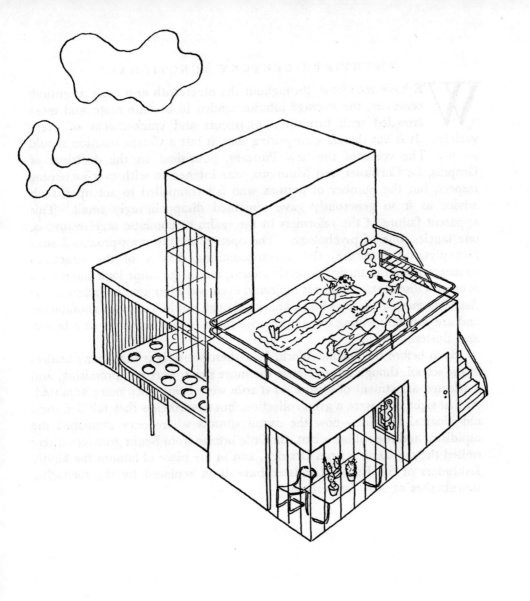

WE have seen how, throughout the nineteenth and early twentieth centuries, the average interior tended to become more and more crowded with furniture, ornaments and knick-knacks of every variety. It is not therefore surprising that at last a violent reaction should set in. The voice of the new Puritans, nourished on the doctrines of Gropius, Le Corbusier and Mumford, was listened to with ever-increasing respect, but the number of persons who felt compelled to act upon such advice as it so generously gave remained disappointingly small. This apparent failure of the reformers in the realm of domestic architecture is, one fancies, one of psychology. The open plan, the mass-produced steel and plywood furniture, the uncompromising display of the structural elements, are all in theory perfectly logical, but in the home logic has always been at a discount. The vast majority, even including many readers of the *New Statesman*, crave their knick-knacks, though not in Victorian abundance, and are perfectly willing to pay the price in prolonged activities with broom and duster.

Even before the Second World War there were signs that many leaders of the school, though not of course the more strict, were compromising, and a selected assortment of *objets d'art et vertu* were being once more admitted. At first sight they were a grim collection, but nevertheless they fulfilled their old illogical function—now the cactus sprouts where once flourished the aspidistra and the rubber-plant, the little bronze from Benin grimaces where smiled the shepherdess from Dresden, and in the place of honour the kindly Labradors of Sir Edwin Landseer have been replaced by the menacing thornbushes of Mr. Sutherland.

WHEN Monsieur Le Corbusier first propounded his theory of the house as a *machine à habiter* it may be doubted whether he foresaw the exact form in which it would first be translated into fact. That other well-known architectural authority, Herr Hitler, must claim the credit for the temporary compliance on the part of the insular British with the extreme dictates of the continental functionalists. Here we saw the bare bones of structure unconcealed save by a flood of interesting and stimulating instructions from the Town Council, the Home Office, the Head Warden, the Fire Brigade, Old Uncle John Anderson and all. Here all attempt at applied decoration, apart from an occasional rude drawing of a pouchy-eyed, middle-aged paranoiac with a tooth-brush moustache (that rapidly attained purely totemistic significance) was abandoned and exclusive reliance was placed on the inherent decorative qualities of corrugated iron and unbleached canvas.

IN the ten years that elapsed between the slump and the erection of Rockefeller Centre, the first of the new-style skyscrapers, a great change had come over American architecture. Shortage of cash led to a general abandonment of the more expensive forms of ornament and decoration, and fortunately the Bauhaus boys, recently arrived in Connecticut from Dessau, were on hand to assure the customers that this development was not only economically advisable but morally and æsthetically right. Structural truth at all costs was their motto and all buildings which attempted to conceal the true nature of their construction, or to disguise the materials in which they were carried out, stood convicted of acting a lie. That a high proportion of the buildings which many generations of mankind had agreed to regard as masterpieces failed to reach this exalted standard was held to be quite irrelevant.

Unfortunately the new theory did not in practice prove quite so easy to carry out satisfactorily as had been hoped. Simplicity is not invariably and on every occasion a virtue, and while desperate attempts to lend some transient interest to a hopelessly uninspired structure by a top-dressing of cornice and pilasters are doubtless highly reprehensible, the bright, unvarnished truth tends too often to be even more depressing. After all few of us, by and large, look our best in the nude.

It is encouraging, therefore, that so many of the more recent skyscrapers have, on the whole, managed successfully to avoid the ultimate in boredom achieved by the United Nations Building. Nevertheless, they only do so by means which the Founding Fathers of Functionalism would have regarded with profound misgiving; by covering those tricky bits between the floors with coloured glass, and by the introduction of returns and setbacks unjustified by the practical requirements of the site.

However, the best of these recent blocks do manage, which so many of the earlier skyscrapers did not, to achieve an effect proportionate to their size. Several acres of steel and glass checkerboarding are rendered lively by the seemingly endless repetition of similar units, which in a lesser space would seem monotonous and inert, seen in constantly changing perspective over a vast façade. Unfortunately in London a lesser space is all that is permitted and the present half hearted adoption of the American style is likely to leave such areas as Knightsbridge and Wigmore Street far more depressing than they were before. For even Cheops was not so unimaginative as to erect a small pyramid, and no structure in the world is less effective than the poor man's skyscraper.

174

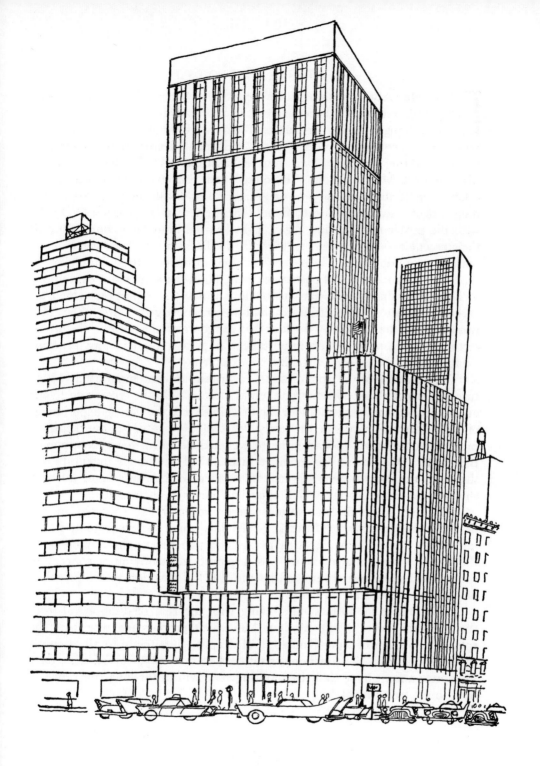

IN the relatively flourishing days before the Second World War, austerity and restraint had seemed to the most advanced school of architectural thought highly desirable, if barely attainable, ideals. Rigidly imposed by economic necessity and government decree, their attractions proved, in the not very long run, exhaustible. Thus when, in 1951, Mr. Herbert Morrison said " Rejoice," and restrictions were waived in celebration of the conclusion of one of the most disastrous centuries in our rough island story, architects found themselves in a quandary. Faced with the problem of striking a gay, light-hearted note, they found little in their recent experience, and still less in the faith in which they had been reared, to guide them. Debarred by their principles from indulging in those frivolous pastiches of past styles, which had made previous exhibitions so agreeable, they strove hard to achieve fitness for a purpose which an earlier generation of doctrinaires had never envisaged. And their task was rendered the harder by the fact that in the Festival of Britain the architectural setting possessed an importance far greater than in any previous exhibition as there were virtually no exhibits.

The influence of the 1951 Festival of Britain on contemporary architecture was out of all proportion to its actual success. On the credit side colour once more returned to façades for the first time since the daring experiments of Mr. Halsey Ricardo in the early years of the century : the Teutonic preponderousness which had hitherto weighed down so many examples of the Modern Movement was modified or banished, and much ingenuity was shown in the employment of such materials as chicken-wire and asbestos sheeting for purposes for which they had never been intended.

All these successful innovations were promptly incorporated in the design of the large blocks of working-class flats which started to go up in the mid-fifties. In addition, in a desperate effort to relieve the monotony of the façade a terrifying ingenuity was displayed in modifying or concealing the basic chequer-board imposed by the L.C.C.s devotion to the principle of absolute residential equality.

While one is far from sympathizing with the roar of disapproval from the ancestral voices of the Modern Movement prophesying woe from the splendid isolation of New Canaan, and deeply sympathetic to all attempts to break out from the functional strait-jacket, one may, nevertheless, dare to express a faint hope that the resulting style will in the long run prove to have been transitional.

N

FEW of the many architectural innovations introduced towards the end of the last century was so long and widely welcomed as the " open plan " of which the late Sir Edwin Lutyens was, perhaps, the most distinguished exponent. Freed from the conventional lay-out imposed by the classical façade, the architect was at liberty, anyhow on an open site, to concentrate on convenience and allow the outward appearance of the house to be largely determined by the internal arrangement. He could, as it were, start on the inside and work out.

Stimulating and advantageous as was the freedom conferred by the new doctrine, when it is pushed to extremes as, in recent years particularly in Scandinavia and the U.S.A., it has been, the results tend to be immediately remarkable rather than permanently satisfying. Cantilever construction, which relieves the walls of any supporting function, the informal style of modern garden lay-out, first introduced by Miss Jekyll, and the rapid development of central-heating and air-conditioning, all combined to render possible the complete abolition of any old-fashioned distinction between indoors and out. To make the total confusion of his client doubly sure the architect did not hesitate to face the inside of his walls with rough-cast and ashlar, and vigorously encouraged the cultivation of ivy, philodendra and other climbing plants upstairs, downstairs and in my lady's parlour.

Any out-of-date concern for privacy was firmly disregarded and every householder was looked on as a potential exhibitionist ready to perform even the most intimate acts beneath the interested scrutiny of any neighbour with a good pair of fieldglasses, happy in the knowledge that at long last he was really at one with the surrounding landscape.

The compensating advantages that went with this condition of permanent exposure were held chiefly to reside in the ability always to enjoy the ever-changing pageant of nature as revealed through the acres of vita-glass which had replaced the all too solid walls that had enclosed less privileged generations. Unfortunately, of course, this remained in practice relatively unexploited owing to the necessity for drawing all the curtains in order fully to enjoy the ever-changing pageant of television.

"WE needs must love the simplest when we see it." This happy
fallacy from which the propagandists for pure-functionalism
had, during the late 'thirties, derived so much comfort and
justification was not, as a slogan, calculated to maintain its power in a
period of enforced austerity. When individual choice was limited over a
long period to the severely restricted " utility " field, the longing for frills
became naturally irresistible. It was gratified in two ways.

The rigid and puritanical functionalism of the Modern Movement
was modified in the immediate post-war period by a movement, called for
reasons which it would be too tedious, and unprofitable, exhaustively to
investigate, the " New Empiricism." In effect this meant, first an inside-
out tendency whereby interior walls were treated as though they were called
upon to withstand the icy buffetings of Connecticut gales ; second by a
desperate attempt to modify the machine-turned efficiency of the " planned "
interior by the introduction of innumerable exotics from jungle and swamp.
This botanical enthusiasm in due course succeeded in modifying not only
the decoration but even the structure of the Modern Home. Curious
wooden grilles appeared, inexplicably jutting out at right angles into the
logical living-rooms of Gothenburg and New Canaan, up which ivy and
philodendron were lovingly trained. The cacti of the Middle European
'thirties were now outclassed by extraordinary growths, conceived on the
Amazon and nurtured in the hothouses of Copenhagen. The Paul Klee
water-colours, the Henry Moore drawings, the *objets trouvés* (picked up
at Shanklin but reminiscent, it was hoped, of the vision of Paul Nash)
were but dimly discernible through the tangled undergrowth ; and faint
traces of liquid manure, too generously applied, rendered tacky the pages
of *Encounter*.

THE second avenue of escape from logically justified austerity led, not to the jungles of the Amazon, but straight back to great-aunt Harriet's front parlour. At a time when necessity, rather than choice, drew a large number of would-be home furnishers into the sale-rooms, the despised and rejected domestic equipment of the Victorian home enjoyed a new vogue. Acquired, in the first place, on the grounds of economy, so strong was the character of these pieces that like a faint touch of garlic, they completely transformed almost any interior into which they were introduced. In due course one Victorian work-table almost inevitably heralded the arrival of a whole summer of ottomans, Aubussons, bead-work fire-screens, Martin engravings, lustres, portières and Bohemian glass engraved with views of the casino at Marienbad.

With such an influx the plain colour-washed walls of an earlier period were obviously out of place, and the survival of the wall-paper industry was assured. By the provision of immensely heavy mounts and deep frames the at first sight so irreconcilable sketches of Messrs. Sutherland and Moore were skilfully acclimatized. And in the 'fifties with the vogue for curly brimmed bowlers, stove-pipe trousers and embroidered waistcoats, even the male inhabitants of these Ouidæsque apartments finally attained an unexpected conformity with their surroundings.

Not the least enjoyable result of this latest development has been the forcing of the older generation, corduroy-clad, *New Statesman*-reading, Freud-reared, into a position of Barrett-like reaction.

JUST as a period of nearly a century elapsed between the final disappearance of the last vestiges of the old rural way of life in 'this country and the maximum development, architecturally speaking, of the cult of Merrie England, so in America it was not until the last cowboy was but a memory for the oldest inhabitants that the myth of the Frontier found widespread expression in architecture. For some years past the higher income brackets have from time to time been accustomed to indulge their pioneer fantasies on dude ranches but it is only quite recently that the ranch-type home has become available in large quantities to the romantic-minded commuters of Long Island and Connecticut. To extol the merits of this novelty the advertising men have coined a new and fascinating set of terms well outside the vocabulary of all previous writers on architecture : —" Split-level," indicating that the inconvenience of two-storeys has at last been successfully combined with the inadequacy of the bungalow; " breezeway," only too accurately summing up the advantages of an open patio between the living-room and " carport " (garage to you) ; " cathedral-ceilinged," which one would like to think presupposed the presence of clustered shafts and lierne vaults but which, alas, almost certainly does not.

While the spectacle of hundreds of these lonely outposts, stretching away eaves to eaves for mile after suburban mile, has a certain macabre fantasy it should not blind us to the fact that as a means of housing an expanding dormitory population the ranch-type home achieves a new high in the uneconomic employment of space. Æsthetically it may well be no worse (and is certainly in its own quiet way no less funny) than the average example of By-Pass Variegated, but it takes up far more room and its builders have deliberately turned their backs on an admirable indigenous small-house tradition (American Basic) such as was not available to their English counterparts when first faced with a similar drastic increase of the urban middle-classes. Even at the risk of involving large numbers of householders in unfortunate traumatic experiences it would seem probable that sooner or later the pressure on *lebensraum*, anyhow on the Eastern seaboard, will involve some drastic action to prevent the indefinite continuance of this architectural Walter Mittyism.

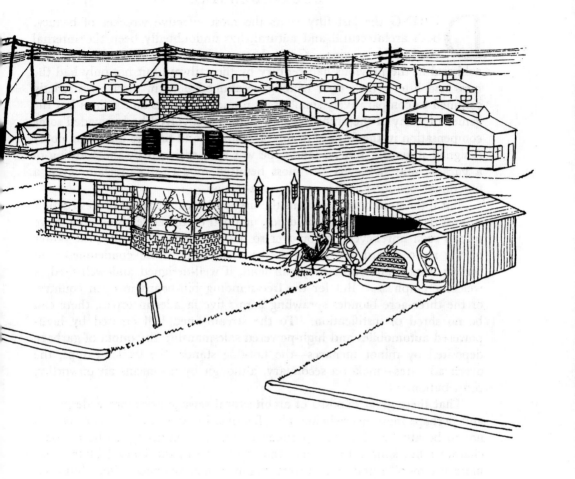

DURING the last fifty years the most effective wrecker of beauty, both architectural and natural, has undoubtedly been the internal combustion engine. Great harm, admittedly, had already been achieved in the previous half-century by the railways but not only had the mess and litter which their coming occasioned been in most cases strictly confined to comparatively small areas round the tracks and sidings but the genius of many of the architects and engineers involved had provided some compensation in the form of dramatic viaducts and bridges and some nobly designed stations. But no landscape was ever enriched by the addition of a garage, and not even the most besotted modernist can claim even a functional beauty for the average gas-station.

But if the automobile remains the first and greatest agent of destruction it must be admitted that it could not, unaided by the advertising man, have spread such unrelieved horror over so wide an area. Not that the poster or the notice-board are in themselves invariably to be condemned ; to certain urban landscapes they can lend, if well-designed and well-sited, a welcome emphasis. But for the free-standing bill-board in open country, or the three-acre blondes sprawling across five façades in towns, there can be no shred of justification. To the stream-lined hell created by high-powered automobiles and high-powered salesmanship the quota of garbage deposited by minor menaces—the hot-dog stands, the trailer camps, the overhead wires—makes a secondary, although by no means an unworthy, contribution.

That these great deposits of architectural sewage are more widespread, and perhaps more overwhelmingly offensive, in America than elsewhere is not to be attributed to any peculiar streak of insensitivity in the national character but simply to the fact that there are in the United States both more automobiles and more advertising men than anywhere else. But even with her comparatively limited resources Europe has achieved some spectacular feats of spoliation, and whole tracts of the Great West Road and the Via Appia are the unquestioned equals of all but the very worst of the American turnpikes.

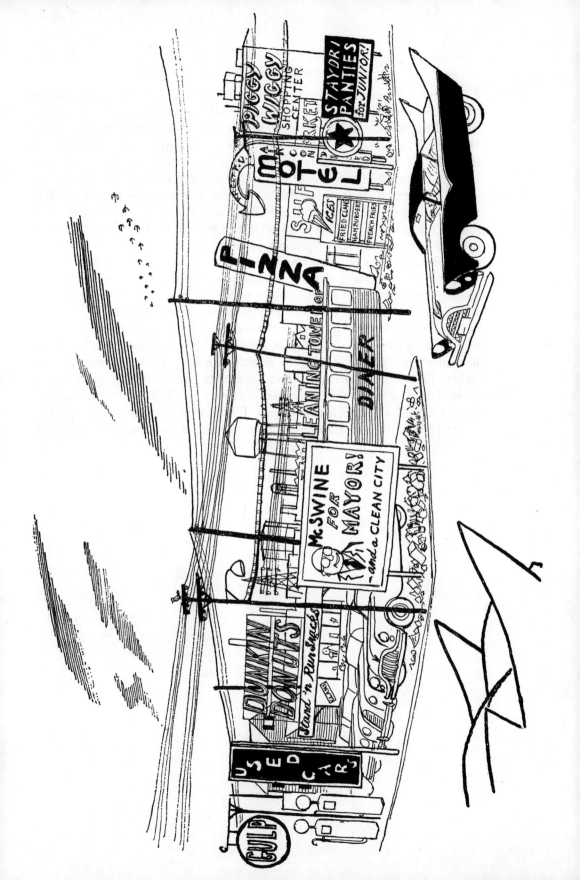

THAT exhausting preoccupation with sex which, from the mid-sixties onwards, earned for the period the label permissive was not without its influence on interior decoration. The chaise-longue, so handy for the casual couplings of Edwardian times, was quite unsuitable for the frenzied, spontaneous copulation of the pop era and the floor was now covered by vast and convenient mattresses usually upholstered in Provençal prints. How frequently, and with what gain in convenience, they fulfilled their erotic purpose is open to question but at least they indicated that, should the possibility of an orgy arise, the hostess was properly equipped.

While some of the action paintings and abstracts so popular in the fifties still remained, they no longer had the walls to themselves and had now to compete with enormous blown-up photographs of those parts of the human anatomy usually classified as 'erogenous zones', and massive enlargements of the hirsute features of celebrated guitarists. Nor were these the only newcomers; from the beginning of the seventies the young were gripped by a strange nostalgic enthusiasm for *Jugendstil*, and more posters by Mucha and Beardsley came off the presses in a month than had ever been printed in the artists' lifetimes. Alongside these, unsuitably marooned on glass-topped tables left over from the functional forties, were Tiffany lamps, Lalique glassware and as large a collection of chryselephantine nudes supporting ash-trays and other such trophies of l'Art Deco, as the owners could afford.

THE hope expressed a few pages back that the style evolved for working-class flats in the mid-fifties would prove to be transitional was not, alas, realised. During the following decades not only did examples increase in numbers but also in size. Working, presumably, on the popular assumption that 'we needs must love the highest when we see it', local authorities, like the rival clans of San Gimigniano, strove with each other to achieve the mastery of the skies, regardless of low-flying aircraft.

Convincing arguments to support this extraordinary procedure were not lacking. With ever-increasing pressure on space the advantages of vertical, rather than horizontal, expansion were clearly obvious; unfortunately the disadvantages only became apparent with time. In theory the space thus saved was to have been devoted to grassy playgrounds and restful gardens but in fact the former were invariably covered in asphalt and the latter rapidly converted into car-parks.

In addition, vertical living was soon found to be attended by certain grave psychological effects. The fact of dwelling either below or above, rather than alongside, one's neighbour, proved, not unforeseeably, to be markedly discouraging to the community spirit, and the feeling of isolation thus induced, combined with the absence of backyards, encouraged the young to find a happy release from claustrophobic boredom in enthusiastic vandalism. Nor was the prevalence of vertigo-induced *angst* among the older generation in any way lessened by occasional mishaps due to an imperfect understanding, on the part of the builders, of the exciting new structural methods and materials made available by modern technology.

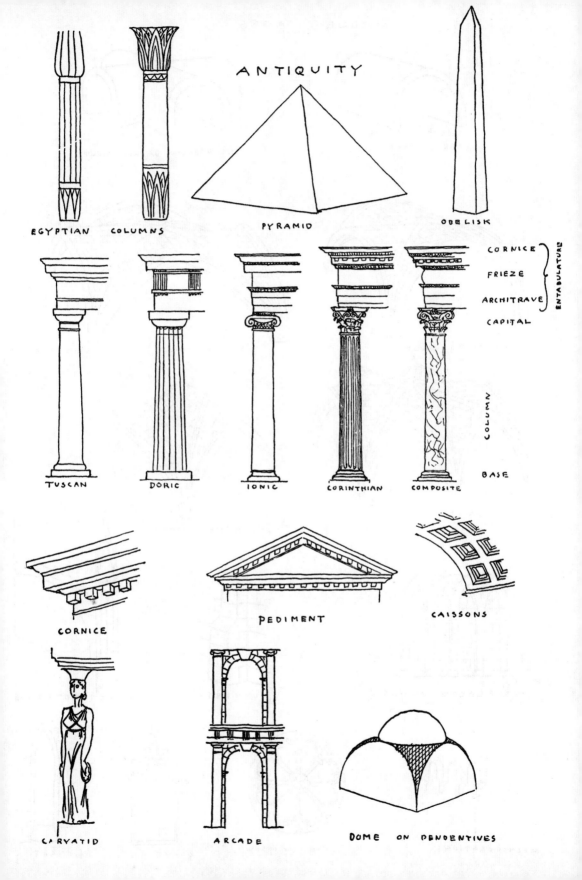

ANTIQUITY

EGYPTIAN   COLUMNS

PYRAMID

OBELISK

CORNICE
FRIEZE
ARCHITRAVE
ENTABULATURE

CAPITAL

COLUMN

BASE

TUSCAN   DORIC   IONIC   CORINTHIAN   COMPOSITE

CORNICE

PEDIMENT

CAISSONS

CARYATID   ARCADE   DOME ON PENDENTIVES

MIDDLE AGES

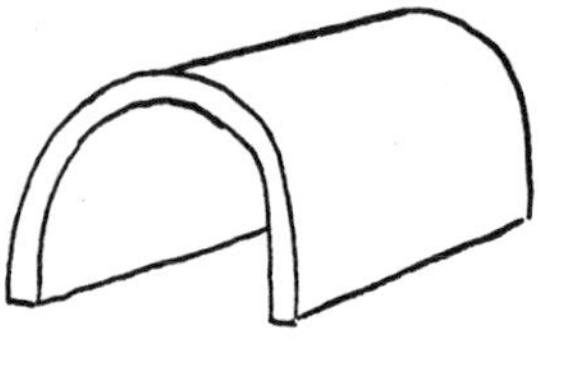

BARREL VAULT

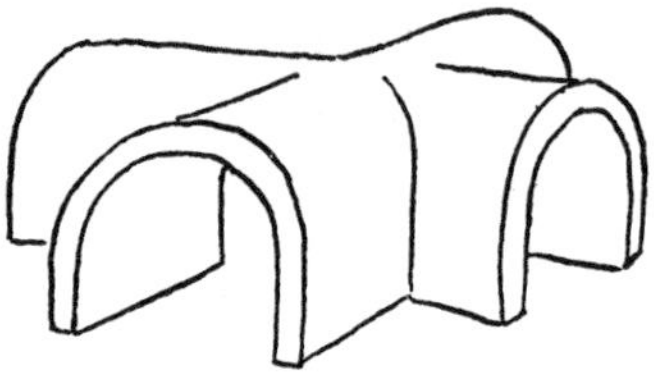

INTERSECTING BARREL VAULTS

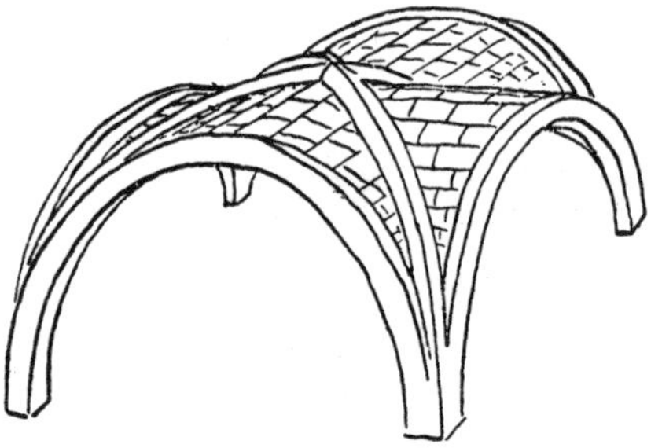

GROINED VAULT

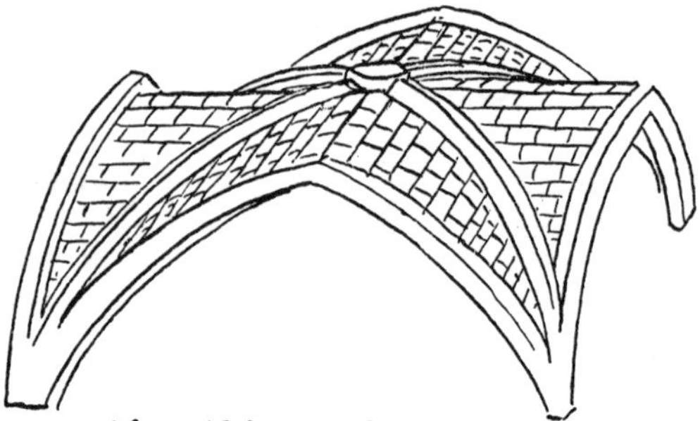

GROINED VAULT ON POINTED ARCHES

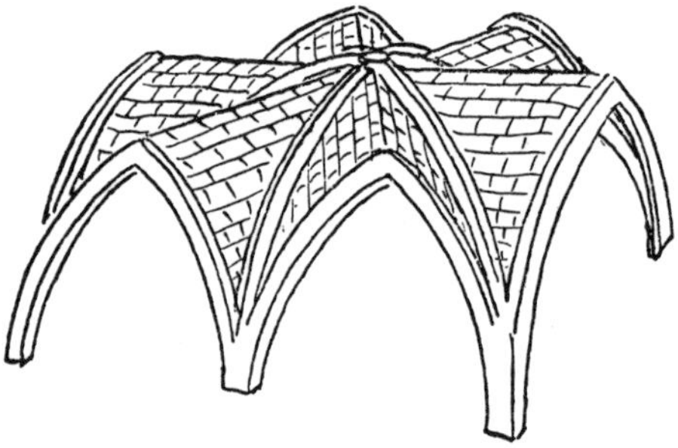

SEXPARTITE VAULT

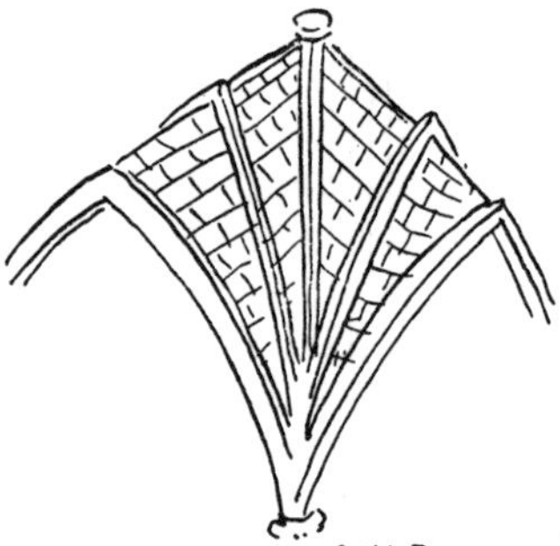

LIERNE VAULT

INTERLACED ARCHES

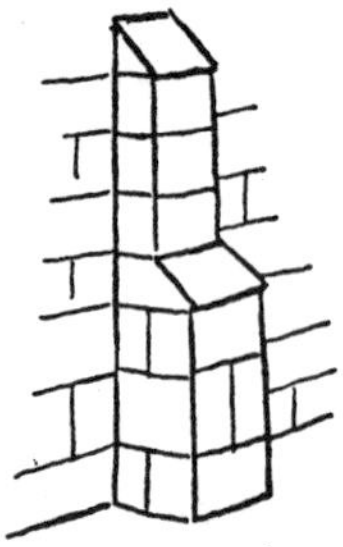

BUTTRESS

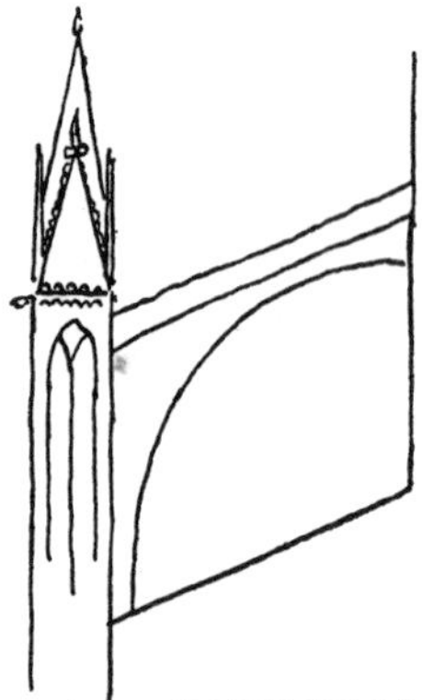

FLYING BUTTRESS

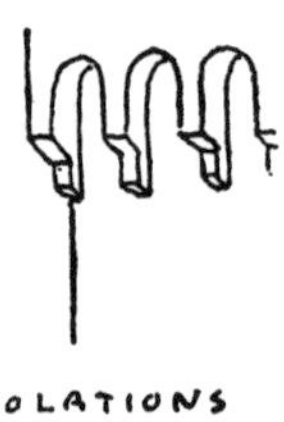

MACHICOLATIONS

ROSE WINDOW

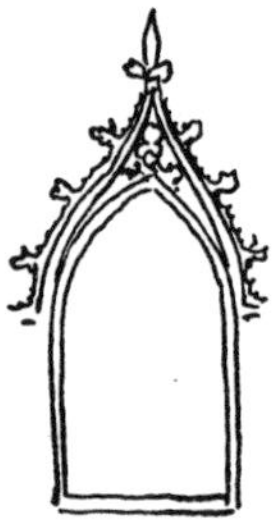

OGIVE

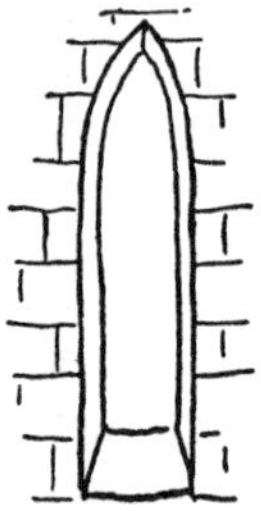

LANCET

RENAISSANCE

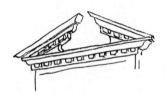

BROKEN PEDIMENT

SEGMENTAL PEDIMENT

CONSOLE

RUSTICATION

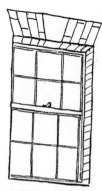

SASH WINDOW

RECESSED ARCH

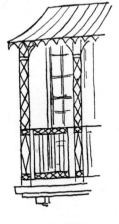

BALCONY

BOW-WINDOW

VENETIAN WINDOW

FAN-LIGHT

DECORATED FRIEZE